SECURITY THEORY

&

KEY PRACTICES

James Lugarkemp

Also by James Lugarkemp

Art Crime and Security

Black Swan Fraud

*'I base my calculation on the expectation
that luck will be against me.'*

Napoleon Bonaparte

PREFACE

All the things you want to remember, none of the things you need to forget.

This book has been written purely with the operational security professional in mind, whether in their security management structure or a team operative. In my twenty five years of experience within the police and security services, as with other professions, you can be inundated with the day to day procedures and protocols, whether written or practical. However, within the realms of the police and security world, one thing became clear to me. That when things go wrong or are going wrong, most of the time you cannot "think the wood for the trees" a term I adopted that has stayed with me, because it is so relevant to security. By that I mean that whatever training you may have had or your years of experience, only the real basics of that training and experience seem to instantly kick in. The important thing to note here, is that those basics will always get you results and will always assist you to accomplish the task at hand. To that extent there is no other book like this on the Amazon marketplace.

That is not to say your broader reading or training does not offer the finer details on individual subject matter, as there are many in this field. However, in this book I have sought to fuse together key practices in daily regulation security activity, because security in its essence is about dealing with people, along with investigation procedure and business continuity, as well as offer a different perspective on terrorism. There are no pictures or charts just the written text, which will serve you as a mini reference book for all you need to know - when it really matters. Always remember to keep up to date with the legal aspects of our profession whatever jurisdiction you are in, as well as making full use of your governmental counter terrorism platforms.

James Lugarkemp

Cambridge

2021

Contents

PART ONE

SECURITY THEORY

CHAPTER 1

Why Security matters and the Theory

As part of my forward to this book my key message was one of simplicity. That is in the way we need to work and our ability to recollect and activate our training when it really matters. But as with any other profession, we need to be aware of our fundamental building blocks, on which all our practical actions are based. Just as importantly, we need knowledge of security theory for two main reasons:

☞ To base all our operational activities on sound security theory

☞ So will are able to speak about the reasons for our practical security decisions and future planning to senior management based on this sound and accepted theory

Given the current state of the world whether in the public or private sector, an organisation of whatever nature or the individual citizen in the street we should all care about security and risk. Because if considered appropriately, proportionately, and acted upon, we would live in a more secure and less risk-averse world. An awareness of risk is completely acceptable because everything we do is risky. Simply by interacting socially or undertaking any enterprise everyone willingly takes risks. Much is made of the concept of Dynamic Risk Assessment and how we are literally assessing risk as soon as we get out of bed in the morning.

However, not all security and risk are conscious or sensible. People will sometimes obsess about certain risks and ignore others. Or manage risks in a distorted way whatever the environment that takes place in. Security is primarily a responsibility for governments. Which acquires military, civilian police, border protection, health authorities, and various regulators for the security of their respective nations in whatever format that takes.

General public expectations for security also continue to grow, considering global issues whether warfare, diplomatic, and most certainly now health. Individual citizens and corporate organisations are expected to take more responsibility for their own security. This in principle is undoubtedly right and governments should always emphasize there is a limit to what they can do. So personal responsibility from the individual citizen, family, private organisation or company is key.

Finally, security thinking has shifted in recent years away from the objectives of security and safety towards a more initiative-taking security and risk management approach, in both the public and private spheres.

That change in thinking has also prompted a desire for more international standardisation so that the many competing and loosely defined ways in which people undertake security and the management of risk can be replaced by best practice.

Better security policy and procedures will therefore promote the following benefits amongst others, albeit these I regard as the key ones, whether in the public or private domains of More Increase and Improve (M2I)

☞ More awareness of security and risk

☞ More initiative-taking ways of working

☞ Increased operational effectiveness and efficiency

☞ Increased compatibility and upgrade of your current practices

☞ Increased compliance with legal and regulatory requirements

☞ Increased opportunities to achieve organisational objectives

☞ Improved organisational (security) culture and resilience

☞ Improved customer confidence and trust

The following three chapters will concentrate on the areas that are the key theory, concepts and building blocks of security; organisational culture, security, risk, hazards, threats, specific targets, organisational capacity and control strategies.

Essentials

- Make sure you can converse about the basics of security theory with anyone

- Security and risk is an everyday part of our lives

- People will sometimes obsess about certain risks and ignore others

- Security has now shifted to a more initiative-taking risk management approach

- That there is a desire for more international standardisation which would provide the benefits of M21

CHAPTER 2

Organisational Culture

Many organisations will now undertake an induction day or make it part of a one/two-week joining course for new employees. Most people are aware of the obligatory course housekeeping of 'this is what you do if there is a fire...' or other standard information supplied along the lines of 'remember security is the responsibility of everyone...don't be afraid to challenge people...' etc.

The reality is people forget all these things the moment they have been said. They think security or fire safety is not a matter for them, that is the security department because that is what they were hired to do. Or when it comes to that moment when they are tailgated through a card access door by someone they do not recognize. How many of them challenge that person? I know what you're thinking so I won't labour the point.

Many organisations in previous years have only ever been concerned with security after an incident has happened, even if that incident does not reflect badly on the organisation. Moreover, most organisations are only concerned with how any investment in security, however badly needed, will affect their bottom line. That is a simple fact.

Employees or visitors to any organisation forget that being security conscious is indeed in their interests. Not just for the company/organisation but for themselves, for their own safety and protection of their personal property when on site. So how can this be rectified?

From my own experience, it only ever happens when it comes right from the very top of an organisation. When those executives have a real appetite for it. When those expectations of being security-minded and of challenging that person walking through the door behind them that they do not recognize becomes a daily occurrence. That those employees not being minded as such will be called to task if a subsequent incident happens that could have been avoided. This effectively then morphs into a culture that comes as standard for any organisation or company because the CEO and his team have become the standard bearers.

Defining Culture

> The Oxford Dictionary of English definition of culture which we would relate to the subject matter is:
>
> *The attitudes and behaviour characteristics of a particular social group*
>
> ...in this case the organisation.

This book is about security theory, so definitions are important as they are a concrete starting point for any discussion. I appreciate there are other sources for definitions, but the idea is to give you a solid source when involved in your own discussions with others and so not get bogged down in the detail of numerous definitions or sources. That is what we are trying to get away from.

Why start Security Theory with Culture?

Because without it we cannot even contemplate bringing a quality security service to an organisation, as you will always be making too many compromises, and conducting security business in a reactive way, not an initiative-taking one. You will always be playing catch up, always papering over the cracks. Most importantly you will go home at night always knowing you could be doing things better but cannot make those instant changes as they are above your pay grade.

Creating an Organizational Culture

Let me make this clear, before you can create and develop an organisational culture you must be able to sell and present it to senior management. Remembering that it must consider the financial bottom line. Culture is easy to neglect but certainly difficult to observe so you need to highlight it...constantly.

However, as a security professional you will have a good idea as to where your organisation is at the present time in terms of the quality of this culture. If an audit is conducted by the security professional, it will identify the root cause or causes. An important example is repeated poor performance by staff during fire alarm tests which indicates a lack of training. Creating and developing a culture is difficult, but initial umbrella solutions include exemplary leadership and more awareness of the desired culture. More rewards for compliance with the desired culture and more punishments for non-compliance, coupled with enforcement by the security team and managers at every cross-departmental level.

Presentation to Management and Staff

Any presentation will of course be fine-tuned by the security management team, with important inputs from all security staff and can be done in conjunction with any current or existing security survey. The security survey will not be discussed in this book as it is an area requiring greater detail and arguably a stand-alone subject.

Security staff and management need to monitor and record daily, for a period of one to three months, any poor attitudes and actions toward security awareness. For example, staff who serially lose or forget their ID/Access cards. One of the most important priorities is to make sure that all staff knows what is required with this culture. Any presentation can be achieved as follows:

- ☞ Prior monitoring, recording, and review by the security department of staff attitudes and actions towards the fundamental security of your organisation

- ☞ Formulating a PowerPoint/video presentation to the CEO and senior management/board of directors of an appropriate time scale, as these people are very busy

☞ Include in that presentation in simplistic terms, as Q and A's will follow, examples and figures from your monitoring, recording, and existing security arrangements not being adhered to. Current national threat levels, examples of recent incidents in your specific organisational commercial sector, and key explanations that a security orientated culture does not affect the bottom line. In fact, it protects it

☞ Ensure that security is a key consideration in future planning and training. This must be done in periods of calm and stability

☞ Make security an agenda item on all senior board meetings with reports (executive style summaries) forwarded from security management to keep busy CEOs up to speed

☞ Making sure that all staff are familiar with the context, risks, commitments, and reasons for the organisation having this new organisational security-based culture

☞ Stipulate the expectations required from middle/departmental managers under normal and high-stress circumstances

☞ Making sure that all other staff are very clear about their individual responsibilities regarding security, with absolutely no compromise

Essentials

- Culture is the foundation for the safety of an organisation and its employees

- A new culture and its effectiveness will only ever work if it comes from the very top and is made clear that they are the instigators

- It does not affect an organisation's bottom line, it protects it

- A presentation needs to be made to the board/senior management to emphasis this new culture is a win...win

- Importance should be placed on the consequences for employees of non-compliance with disciplinary action for repeat offenders

CHAPTER 3

Security, Risk, Hazards and Threats

This section is concerned with the concept of security and its origins which are in risk, hazards, and threats. Security as a term is often used in combination with safety, health, defence, and protection whether it be in the public domain, corporate or individual citizen. There has been much written about how security is described at different levels whether it be in academia, national or international security levels, or now very much in worldwide human health issues.

Regardless of the variation in meanings of security, they are inextricably linked with the concepts of risk, hazards, and threats. The aim of this section is to consolidate all these key concepts, as they are the only real and universally acknowledged basis of all security theory and practice and the only ones that really matter.

Security

There are numerous definitions of the concept of security, many of which are long-winded and elaborate. The following definition covers everything in its simplicity and underpins our profession:

Security = Freedom from Risk

Security can, therefore, be described as the inverse of those associated sources of risk, hazards and threats. Each having implications for the other with risk always emanating from hazards and threats. Those numerous definitions of security that can be found in books and articles about our profession, generally come from the following sources: the UN, NATO, and various nation-states such as the United States, Britain, Canada, and the EU. These can be easily obtained and read but I promise you that you will get bogged down in the detail. Importantly, security operates on many levels:

☞ Individual Citizen

☞ Family

☞ Local

☞ City/Town

☞ Provincial

☞ Federal

☞ National

☞ Trans-National

It can crossover at any of these levels and indeed moves freely between these levels because it does not necessarily operate in a hierarchy. For example, terrorist activity at a major power station immediately becomes a provincial or federal issue, not just local.

Academically security crosses many domains. It is studied in greater detail only, I suggest, by a mix of disciplines. The main fields being:

- ☞ Criminology

- ☞ Policing

- ☞ Public Safety

- ☞ Health and Medicine

- ☞ Political Science

- ☞ International Relations

- ☞ Military and Defence Studies

- ☞ Economic (including food) Security

- ☞ Counter terrorism

- ☞ Environment

These security levels and academic headings are all you need to be aware of for the purpose our profession. But it will be useful to commit those headings to memory as part of your security theory knowledge on which we base everything and on which we can converse about.

Risk

At this point please do not get confused by discussions that compare and contrast negative and positive risks. Commentators compare and contrast these by using the terms uncertain harm for negative risk and uncertain benefit for positive risk. My view is forget the terms and the comparison. You will find different definitions out there for risk, which is a very simple concept in its day to day practical meaning. Again, forget all these the bottom line is that risk by its very nature is negative and any benefits gained from it are purely a gamble or at its very least, luck.

For example, traders on the stock and money markets. Now my knowledge in this area is virtually zero. However, like most of the citizens on the street I know many of their transactions may carry very little risk. But the bottom line is unless it is money already in the bank or they can easily cover losses and protect profits margins, every transaction is by its very nature a risk. That is basic economics.

It can be defined in a way that keeps us on our guard, as simply:

Risk = The Level of Likelihood of Harm Occurring

The important word to remember here is level as the level of any risk will impact your overall security and response to the risk. The level of any such risk is an organisational decision alone except where legislation and/or regulation needs to be factored in.

Finally, there are types and descriptions of risk. These are important main concepts and need to be committed to memory. The main types or categories are:

☞ Environmental

☞ Political

☞ Social (people made)

☞ Technological

For example, your organisation is moving high-value goods to another location by road in a large vehicle. Security must consider during transit the following:

☞ Weather Conditions

☞ If goods are subject to protester group actions

☞ How vulnerable are they to theft

☞ Delivery reliant on IT documentation which could be hacked

A good understanding of risk, whether organisational or for specific valuable goods and services will help in deciding its agreed level of risk and thus the security measures subsequently decided upon.

The description will consist of:

☞ Scope of the risk

☞ Source of the potential hazard or threat

☞ Probability of a potential incident

☞ The outcome of an incident

For example, the goods we are moving by road which are highly valuable (the scope.) Similar goods are moved every three months and may be subject to theft (hazard/threat.) That means four opportunities every year for the goods to be stolen (probability of an incident.) The goods are worth millions and would be subject to negative publicity if stolen (the outcome of an incident.)

Hazards and Threats

Hazards and threats are the sources of risk and can be defined as:

> *Hazard = something with the potential to cause harm*
>
> *Threat = something that is about to cause harm*

For example, a river that has flooded is a hazard, when that river reaches your street it is now a threat. A group of protestors planning to visit your site that you become aware of, a hazard. These protesters then arrive at your site entrance, they are now a threat. Notice that when you are in the threat zone in these basic examples that threat is now very real.

There is a transition period from hazard to threat like the term Hierarchy of Control used in health and safety, which is the removal of a hazard or its elimination completely. I will not discuss this area any further here as risk analysis will be covered in more detail later. Generally, this transition period can be listed simply as:

☞ Activation

☞ Coincidence

☞ Enablement

☞ Release

Activation means that activity or activities have changed a hazard into a threat. For example, environmental activity by your organisation without first conducting a local resident discussion. Coincidence means exactly that and usually involves the uncontrollable like environmental issues such as weather conditions that are unexpected or change at short notice.

Enablement is like activation but will be more specific. For example, an employee sympathetic to protester activity supplies confidential company strategy information. The release is again straightforward in that it could be something as simple as a chemical held on-site which is ignited causing a fire and substantial damage.

The Black Swan

I do not want to finish this section on security, risk, hazards, and threats without a mention of the Black Swan theory. As security operatives you should always, always, expect the unexpected. Black Swan theory was discussed in the 2007 book The Black Swan by Nassim Nicholas Taleb. He initially undertook his research into unexpected events within financial markets on Wall Street where he worked, but then took his writings into a social context.

The term was derived from (to keep it simple) a 16th century expression that suggested that the black Swan did not exist. Until a Dutch explorer went to Australia and found, you guessed it, black Swans. Taleb advocates that a small number of black swans explain almost everything in our world and to constitute a black swan event they contain three key elements:

☞ Rarity - the event is outside the realm of regularly expected events in the history of the world and all its constituent subject matters i.e., war, science, technology and nothing in the past points to its possibility

☞ Extreme Impact - the event has a major impact with worldwide implications

☞ Rationalised by hindsight - governments and academics then try to explain away the event retrospectively i.e., it was an expected event and there was available data, but it was unaccounted for at the time

An historical, anecdotal if you like, example used by Taleb is the turkey that gets fed for 1000 days and becomes big. The turkey thinks this is its life and every day is predictable. Then on day 1001 the turkey is hit on the head and becomes the focal point of the family dinner table at Christmas. Real life black Swan events suggested by Taleb with monumental effects are the events of 1914, the rise of Hitler, demise of the Soviet bloc, rise of Islamic fundamentalism, the market crash of 1987 and the housing crash of 2008.

So why even mention this theory? Despite the validity of the theory there seem to be many academics who do not agree with it even more so economists. However, it seems to be quite a famous theory that few people seem to know exists. Why do I like it? Because it expresses what we should all be conscious of in the security world and that is to always expect the unexpected. Although the theory is based on large scale catastrophic events rather than our regular daily events, just be aware of the theory as we never know what might happen tomorrow particularly in our profession.

Essentials

- 👉 Security = Freedom from Risk

- 👉 Security operates at various levels from individual citizens to trans-national and can be interlinked

- 👉 Security can only be studied in-depth by the interlinking of various academic disciplines

- 👉 Security is inextricably linked to risk, hazards and threats

- 👉 Risk at a basic level is made up of types (environmental etc) and description (scope etc) of risk

- 👉 There is a transition period from hazard to threat concerning activation, coincidence, enablement, and release whether individually or collectively

- 👉 Remember the black Swan and always expect the unexpected

CHAPTER 4

Specific Targets, Organisational Capacity and Control Strategies

O nce a risk has been identified and acknowledged, concentration should then be focused to identify the potential target and assess its vulnerability and exposure. To achieve this in any plan or security survey/assessment, actual organisational capacity and the required controls are then decided upon.

Specific Targets

Analytically, risk should be identified in relation to a target whether specific or more general i.e., a particular piece of artwork or a whole gallery of artworks. A target is the 'bullseye' of risk. A target can also be a person/group or an event not just an inanimate object. The U.S. Department of Defence I believe offers the simplest and most appropriate definition:

> *Target = an entity or object considered for possible engagement or other action*

Linked in with this will be the vulnerability of the target which would involve assessing the degree of loss/damage or consequences of it. Similarly, exposure would be looking at any loss/damage to a specific target from a more overarching organisational viewpoint.

This would include things such as negative publicity or an inability to secure adequate insurance cover in the future. So, for example that piece of artwork is in a gallery which is now locked during opening hours of a museum. The artwork is not vulnerable whilst the gallery remains locked. However, it is still subject to generalized exposure by its existence in the museum. I will leave these points here whilst they remain simple.

A criteria EVIL DONE (Clarke & Newman 2006 relating to terrorism) which is useful in all contexts for assessing specific target selection and their vulnerability and exposure is as follows with a museum context:

- ☞ Exposed - the artwork is vulnerable i.e., the gallery is open

- ☞ Vital - it is the showpiece of the museum and adds significant revenue

- ☞ Iconic - theft/damage would be subject to extensive publicity

- ☞ Legitimate - it has been subject to previous protester activity

- ☞ Destructible - it can be damaged or destroyed

- ☞ Occupied - the museum is open to the public

☞ Near - to key escape routes i.e., underground station

☞ Easy - to facilitate the actual theft or damage

Organisational Capacity

An organisation's ability to cope with risk is linked with its ability to defend, respond, and recover. Capacity is the potential for an organisation to achieve something. This concept is straightforward and obvious. For example, the military has the capacity to enter a battlefield scenario, the police have highly skilled detectives to investigate any murder. However, the two areas could not be accomplished by both due to the skill set, equipment, and logistics of their respective organisations. A definition of capacity would therefore be:

> *Capacity = the combination of all strengths and resources available to an organisation*

It is important to remember that not all strengths and resources are tangible. For example, an emergency on your organisation's site would only involve security personnel and possibly staff fire wardens. Other staff would not have the skills or training to assist you. Likewise, your building could be used as an emergency storage facility by the authorities because of a nearby incident. However, due to sensitive assets in certain areas, not all of your site would be available to the authorities.

Finally, it can be argued that an increase in capacity does not necessarily mean an increase in security. What is true is that a decline in the capacity of your security can lead to drastic increases in risk. Likewise, increased capacity to facilitate more security will always work, but only if it is combined with increased risk assessment and controls and not just the capacity to respond post-incident.

Control Strategies

Control strategies are key in security theory and are our blueprint of how we have decided to control our organisational risk, whether individual asset decisions or within the overall framework. I sometimes feel at pains to use the word strategy. A word that I believe is overused and a bit too management speak. So, when you hear this word bounded around in the security world or anywhere else, remember, a strategy is just a plan. Thus, it can be defined as:

> *Control Strategy = a planned response intended to reduce a risk*

A control is not necessarily a complete solution to a risk. Your best solution may reduce a risk to acceptable levels or temporarily remove it. So, it follows that your strategy will require ongoing monitoring of the risk even after control. Risk is diverse and organisations need to find their own thresholds for what they will tolerate.

Within security theory numerous concepts overlap and sometimes things seem to be explained in a variety of ways. Things we have seen before but which all lead to the same conclusions and no doubt can be simplified. For example, as previously mentioned there is a hierarchy of controls used in Health and Safety which essentially control hazards. Similarly, with risk there is a similar set of hierarchical controls and these are as follows:

☞ Eliminate the Risk - removing the risk completely will always be a decision for the organisation's board or CEO, as it may be an asset mission critical to your organisation i.e., an iconic piece of artwork in a museum or dangerous chemicals crucial to a production process

☞ Tolerate the Risk - toleration of a risk is invariably a popular choice. This must only be done after full discussion with the security department who need to present the pros and cons of this pathway and hopefully in a fashion that involves compromise on both sides. As opposed to an increase in security capacity, that as we know now, may affect or start to affect an organisation's bottom line

☞ Diversify the Risk - in other words mix things up with assets. For example, only have a limited quantity of the required chemical on site at any one time. Or your museum piece you could decide to only display for limited periods during the day before closing the gallery or a security operatives stand next to it during very busy periods

☞ Transfer the Risk - finally, you can offset the risk for example by way of insurance. This would work better for assets that are expensive but easy to replace i.e., production line components, obviously not irreplaceable artwork

Essentials

- Once a risk has been identified focus should be on the potential target its vulnerability and exposure

- Use the **EVIL DONE** criteria, contextually, to identify your target

- An organisation's capacity is its ability to defend, respond, and recover

- Not all organisational strengths and resources are tangible for the security department

- Effective control methods in security are key and strategy is just a plan

- The fundamental control options are eliminating, tolerate, diversify, and transfer

PART TWO

KEY PRACTICES

CHAPTER 1

Key Security Practices
know the basics well

As alluded to in the first section of this book building blocks are very important in our profession, but not always easy to recall. There are a lot of crossover concepts and theory but also a lot of information on the actual key practices. These can become complicated by too much overlap with other practices and full of management speak.

The following section will again cut through all that. We will concentrate on all the essentials and mention other areas that are important, whilst remembering this is all about what you need, when you need it most. The final section deals with how we conduct ourselves as security operatives within the bigger picture and how we are generally perceived by other people in our organisations.

The section will cover the main areas of management of risk, perimeter and building security and integrated systems such as CCTV and alarms as well as investigations conducted by security operatives and your role in crisis management and business continuity. This will be done in the context of your everyday practical remit on site, not just a discussion in a theory type style or regarding equipment specifications, because this will not help you in those crucial times or when you do not want to make day to day mistakes or overlook issues.

Examples will be given of how you the security operative take your day-to-day security theory and practices and mould them into an efficient and effective way of working. Thinking about them and applying them every day whilst patrolling or looking at organisational assets, people, and visitors, this will be your daily practical revision as you work. It will consolidate your knowledge and be in your mind when you need it most.

CHAPTER 2

Security Risk Management

Risk Analysis and Risk Mitigation

Let me be clear from the start, risk management in our profession is reliant on two simple acts daily by you and your organisation: Risk Analysis and Risk Mitigation. I use these terms to differentiate between those used by us, in security risk management, and those similar terms used in Health and Safety. So please always use our terms but remember them in this way. Risk analysis is a simple risk assessment of your assets, people and visitors daily by you, colleagues, and the organisation. Risk mitigation are the controls applied to assets, people, and visitors daily by the security department or organisation, which will be subject to daily or periodic review and modification.

There are also two other key factors to remember in an overarching way. Firstly, treat your security department, yourself, and close colleagues as a unit of the organisation. With the central aim to provide a service that contributes to the overall well-being of the organisation. It must integrate with the organisational vision, mission, and objectives and not be a simple internal policing function. A security department functioning properly within an organisation can only be achieved with cross-departmental consent and compromise and needs to be positive and initiative-taking. Secondly, a word on Standard Operating Procedure (SOP) and Assignment Instructions (AI.) These are the bread-and-butter documents in the security world on which all your security risk analysis and mitigation will be based. These should be in a manual in your manager's office which is accessible to you and other authorised staff.

It is the key document - the bible - on which the entire security blueprint is based for your organisation telling you exactly how to keep your organisation and its employees safe. When you arrive in new employment this particular security bible should exist and be available for you to read immediately. If it does not exist be afraid, and maybe seek other employment sooner rather than later. Your own personal reputation may rest upon it.

This part of the book is all about us and how we work daily. Thinking about the risks to assets, people and visitors as well as lateral risks or issues. The key here is to keep asking yourself what if? questions. Here are the three key security building blocks that provide the practical fundamentals to all our security risk management concerns.

PDCA

We can use a variation of the simple, International Organisation for Standardisation (ISO) four-point plan, PDCA, to do our own personal daily assessments and monitoring. If we believe security issues are discovered, we can then report back immediately to our security manager(s.)

- ☞ Plan - exam a potential security issue, an asset or otherwise

- ☞ Do - decide what the issues are and think of a solution

- ☞ Check - confirm your assessment and put in writing to your line supervisor/manager

- ☞ Act - monitor any new mitigation that is implemented

From the above you can see how a standardized form of risk analysis and mitigation can be undertaken at a personal level. Bear in mind unless it is an obvious risk needing immediate action, your assessment can be done over a period suitable for you to undertake the planning and do part of the assessment by assessing daily and seeing if the risk has variations.

Data Protection

As security operatives we should all be aware of the importance of data protection and that laws vary worldwide. For example, there is the General Data Protection Regulation (GDPR) 2018 in Europe and mainly federal based laws in the USA. In Europe Human Rights law is the overarching legislation for GDPR. Everything that is written down in the security world will invariably have an impact on your organisation and in some shape or form involve the protection of data. As of 2018, the GDPR will take effect regardless of Brexit and is focused on the data subjects themselves. By contrast the US does not seemingly apply the same citizen first approach to handling and protection. There are some sector or state orientated approaches to data protection mostly concerning healthcare companies or financial institutions. But whilst data protection is expansive it can be argued laws in the US are not as stringent as those concerning countries in the EU.

Regardless of whether we are considering jurisdictional laws, I suggest the following summary be applied by you in your work on a day to day basis. Supporting your organisation's requirements of data protection by remembering the following seven rules on data protection as you encounter data daily:

1. The processing of data must be lawful

2. And for a specific purpose

3. And then only data which is necessary

4. This data new (or already stored but updated) must be accurate

5. This data should be deleted when no longer required

6. This data should be processed and stored in a secure way

7. The designated data controller is accountable for all the above

Commit the following line to memory, it is a key security responsibility and will also involve monitoring and enforcement by your department.

> *Lawful-Specific-Necessary-Accurate-Deleted-Secure-Accountable*

Onion Skin and 4D's

Conscious not to overlay or over complicate all our areas and practical application of security measures when considering our day-to-day risk monitoring, we need to do that within a generic framework. This will be centred around our own PDCA and GDPR work. This generic framework will involve the 'onion skin' approach and the 4D's of security.

Our key security practices are all encompassed with the basic consideration of what we have been asked to protect by our organisation. However, all protection will involve defence-in-depth. Often known as layered security but easily remembered as the 'onion skin' approach. Thus, layers of skin that become harder to overcome as you near your key asset(s.) Layers are best explained by using the 4D's:

1. Deny - strong physical components, fencing, lighting, barriers

2. Delay - locking doors, access control

3. Detect - CCTV, all alarm systems, security patrols

4. Defend - response/apprehension by operatives

Tests and Drills

For your security department and more importantly your organisation, to be effective in security risk management, and feed that all important security culture staff tests and drills must be conducted periodically. I cannot emphasize how important this is because practice makes perfect. This is different from daily monitored operations, but very important and essential for spontaneous events such as security breaches, fire alarms and hardware/software failures. The tests and drills can include:

- ☞ Scenarios/Drills - such as fire or other evacuation with agreed upon frequency and debrief

- ☞ Tabletop exercises - such as bomb threats or Invacuation with problem solving and Q and A's included

- ☞ Penetration Testing - using external actors who provide feedback. With testing undertaken without security staff knowledge of any test and for the benefit of security operatives only

Essentials

- ➤ **The core parts of security risk management are risk analysis and risk mitigation**

- ➤ **Every single organisation or facility should be in possession of Security Assignment Instructions (AI)**

- ➤ **You need to think about and assess your organisation's assets, people and visitors daily**

- Do this by using PDCA and GDPR within the Onion Skin and 4D's framework, that way you cover all the angles, every day

- Absolutely nobody is any good at anything unless they practice, tests and drills must be part of the AI and organisational culture

CHAPTER 3

Perimeter, Building Security and Lighting

This chapter will look at our bricks and mortar security needs and our role within it. Looking at any security type perimeter, then our buildings all integrated with our security lighting. I will again look at the practicalities of what we should be aiming to achieve and undertake daily. At this point in the book I will diversify, that is to say take from the remaining chapters what is relevant to you and remember it/use it as required.

CP-TED

There is a defining concept we need to be aware of that is important when looking at perimeter, building and lighting security. It is a familiar, but relevant concept called Crime Prevention Through Environmental Design, commonly known as CP-TED in the UK. For me it is a key framework when you are thinking and observing daily perimeter, building security and lighting at your facility. Part of any mitigation strategy (plan) should include CP-TED. The concept refers to the design, upkeep, and management of the built environment of your facility. It is made up of four building blocks I call MONA:

1. Mechanical - i.e., barriers, walls

2. Organisational – i.e., security office management

3. Natural – i.e., trees

4. Architectural – i.e., building design

When considering building security at any facility, your organisation should have (or is) considered the five CP-TED principles:

☞ Natural surveillance - this is the placement of windows and pathways allowing for observation by security or any employee

☞ Natural access control - use of physical barriers, channel/guide visitors through the site environment i.e., pathways/parking zones

☞ Territorial reinforcement - i.e., bollards that demarcate public streets to facility entrance areas, allowing for early detection

☞ Maintenance and management - ensuring a facility is well maintained reduces the risk of criminality. The Broken Window Theory (Wilson & Kelling) 1982

☞ Target hardening - the upgrading of doors and window locks, CCTV etc. will have a deny and detect affect which aligns with our four D's in risk management

Perimeter Security

Perimeter security i.e., fencing is your first line of defence to your facility in the onion skin with four D's principle. I am not going to discuss fencing. Rather, the layers that can then be applied inside the perimeter itself complimenting the onion skin include:

- ☞ Access control points (ACP's)

- ☞ Vehicle Searches

- ☞ Clear zone

- ☞ Perimeter intrusion detection system (PIDS)

- ☞ Closed circuit television (CCTV)

- ☞ Perimeter security lighting

- ☞ Security patrols in the zone

Once you have looked (remember you are now using this book to take a fresh look at what you do as a security operative daily - I will not repeat this point again) at your facility perimeter and considered its appropriateness, you can now think about what you need to do in your role as an operative.

Access Control Point

The main point of vulnerability for your perimeter will be your main ACP's. This may seem obvious, but it is a key point. A perimeter may be defeated in two main ways, deceit via the access point i.e., stolen access pass or tailgating whether vehicle or pedestrian without activating security systems at that time. Physical force by breaking through with no concern for detection i.e., protester activity both night and day.

ACP's are the perimeters most vulnerable points, and you will most certainly have more than one. They are normally controlled by gates, barriers and turnstiles and these points need to be kept to a minimum in number. They will no doubt be covered by CCTV even if you have an operative posted at this location. As the CCTV operative this is where you need your best concentration. Not just because of tailgaters but because of employees letting people through after a short conversation and just assuming these people will report to security regards that conversation and their actions of allowing another person access to the site. Do not be the one that misses this on CCTV. Always work together with security colleagues to eradicate any vulnerability at ACP's, whether they be at the location or you call operatives to attend the location to put in a challenge.

Vehicle Searches

I will mention at this point vehicle searches at ACP's, to avoid subject matter crossover as much as possible in later chapters. In relation to vehicles searches know what you are doing and make sure your training is refreshed on a regular basis. People watch you search their cars your thief and protesters may be able to view your ACP from a distance and watch your search protocols. In my years of experience in the police and security environment I have conducted numerous vehicle searches, they are a different set of criteria from searching people.

Seems obvious, but the following method is simple, safe, effective, easy to remember and covers you from any allegations of wrongdoing by the person or their vehicle being searched (who for the purpose of searching I have always referred to as the subject.) Use the following method but make sure the subject is alerted before arrival at your facility that their vehicle will be searched if applicable to your AI.

☞ Stop the vehicle in your designated search area, CCTV should be monitoring you. Ask the subject to turn off the ignition and step out of the vehicle with their keys, which they retain. It is then more difficult to jump back into the vehicle with the keys already in the ignition with a turn only needed to restart the engine

☞ Explain the process of the requirement of the search and the search procedure itself. This may or may not include looking at the engine block or using an under-vehicle inspection mirror as per AI

☞ Before the search, ask them what is inside the seated areas/glove compartment(s) of the vehicle and what is in the boot (trunk.) If they are not sure, ask them why they do not know i.e., it is a pool car for their company, and they have not looked

☞ As you conduct the search, require the subject to open all doors, glove compartment(s), boot (engine hood) for you and that they observe your search/sweep

☞ Sweep the seated areas and glove compartment(s) using a small torch even in daylight as this helps. Then search the boot/trunk making sure you examine all areas around the spare wheel (if located in the boot area.) Conduct engine/mirror checks if applicable

☞ Advise subject search is completed and thank them for their cooperation, record the search or advise your security office

Remember the above as this and do it every time the exact same way.

> *Ignition, subject, keys - explain, ask, require - observed, sweep, search - Record*

Clear Zone

Your clear zone is behind the perimeter fence or between fences. It provides for early detection as per the CP-TED natural surveillance principle and thus allows time to monitor CCTV and provide the best response. So, daily make sure you observe your clear zone on a regular basis whether by CCTV or on your patrols.

Perimeter Intrusion Detection System

Your PIDS are key in detecting an attempt/breach of your perimeter into your clear zone. I would suggest this system would be used mainly at night in the form of a complete system locking down the outside of your facility, or during the day around sensitive assets within your facility perimeter. The choice of PIDS by your security managers will be based on security analysis and mitigation choices in your AI but usually take on three forms; fence mounted units, maybe sound sensitive, free-standing units maybe active infra-red or buried units which are pressure sensitive.

I mention the PIDS system because again they are a key perimeter system, and you need to be aware of them and what they do and how they function. In your daily work you should make sure these are not damaged or been/being interfered with by a visitor unintentionally, i.e., people leaning against a free-standing unit. Or a fence unit that has been accidentally knocked. That they have not been obstructed i.e., by a colleague who has moved a barrier inadvertently blocking a beam line. Or that a buried unit is indeed still buried and not showing through the ground i.e., in a grass area where earth may have naturally moved. These need checking every day on your patrols or if the problem is identified via CCTV.

CCTV

Your use of closed-circuit television CCTV is key specifically when considering your perimeter security. For this you must remember camera considerations are most important. Your organisation should have the entire perimeter in field of view 24/7. On your perimeter extra fixed cameras should be used to fill any identified gaps, as too many pan tilt and zoom cameras (PTZ) will compromise the integrity of your perimeter if it is moved and then not re-positioned back.

As a security operative thinking about perimeter CCTV, you should remember to do the following. Do not rely on colleagues to constantly monitor perimeter CCTV, do your patrols. Get to know your camera types and their location coverage, do this by using the CCTV and patrolling the perimeter and observing the cameras and their masts. From this you can also report any damage to cameras, lens cleaning requirements or cameras which are no longer in the correct position and need physical adjustment i.e., fixed cameras.

Security Lighting

Your security lighting is a key pillar for your CP-TED requirements but is often overlooked or poorly catered for compared to fencing or alarms. It will need to reflect the nature of your facility perimeter considering relevant installation and local/national guidelines such as light pollution, but more on that later. As you move around your facility after sunset or during the night you should be checking the following to make sure your perimeter lighting is complimenting your CCTV and PIDS.

Perimeter lighting should be on the perimeter line illuminating outside the perimeter, but not the inside. Make sure this is the case, via CCTV or patrols, that your immediate clear zone area after the perimeter is properly in darkness. This is a major deterrent to any encroachment. That lighting from the perimeter also provides sufficient illumination to your building facilities and other relevant areas this aspect is best checked on your patrols. That movement detectors illuminate floodlights for intruder detection and are working by walking those areas specifically to activate those lights. Finally, whether operating CCTV or patrolling during the hours of darkness the operative should always be aware of the following:

- ☞ Emergency lighting provided by back-up systems i.e., emergency power generator for any power failure, is fully functioning

- ☞ Warm-up and strike times of lighting at the perimeter

- ☞ Perimeter lighting quality/rendition is conversant with your CCTV

Patrols

Your perimeter patrols will provide a key compliment to all other perimeter security measures, because patrols at your perimeter are your biggest security mitigation. The mere presence of the security operatives is invaluable. But remember this, your patrols are only effective if they are random. Never underestimate that you are being watched by the potential thief or protester as they undertake their reconnaissance. Remember during your patrols to check on all the other elements of your perimeter security as above. Be initiative-taking during the hours of darkness but randomly conduct these activities. Record perimeter patrols and any potential issues encountered and make sure you do a proper patrol handover briefing.

Finally, make sure you can liaise effectively with emergency services/law enforcement at your perimeter. This may not just be about your facility, but it may be about an unrelated incident outside of your facility. The ability to liaise with the authorities should form part of any security operative training package and will be of help to you when you need it most. Guidance should also be available in your AI.

Essentials: Perimeter

- **Perimeter security should be based on the principles of CP-TED**
- **ACP's are the main points of vulnerability for your perimeter security**
- **Search vehicles the same way, every time**
- **Layers should be implemented just behind your perimeter complimenting the onion skin and 4D's framework**
- **Always check the condition of your PIDS and perimeter lighting via CCTV and patrols**
- **Patrols on your perimeter should always be random, you never know who might be watching**

Building Security

Threats to your facility building(s) will range from thieves, contractors, delivery people, employees, protesters, and visitors. Your organisation's AI will identify the core threats and adversaries. Unlike perimeter security, the actual security and safety of your building can only be achieved with a combination of the onion skin and 4D's principle and an organisational security culture. People are key here and thus our organisational building security can only be achieved by; people, culture, the onion skin/4D's, searching of persons entering your building and additional technical measures. It can be argued that to achieve a proper security culture you need to employ the right people from the outset. In my experience this just does not happen. Generally, employees do not care, why? because they are so tied up with their own day to day jobs that they forget about it. Many of them too are like shrinking violets because it may involve them challenging their fellow employees which God forbid might create some tension.

However, as the security operative we should and always will hold the higher ground for when things go wrong and when there is a subsequent internal/external enquiry. So, remember the following in relation to buildings:

☞ An organisation as a bare minimum has a Health and Safety obligation/duty of care in its building(s) to provide a safe place of work. Classic example, fire evacuation procedures

☞ Your bible, your AI, have told you how you need to implement risk analysis and risk mitigation in every aspect of the organisation

☞ It can only ever be properly achieved by an organisational culture of security, which all employees are informed about from their initial joining induction or continuous input from department managers

So, as you can see, we as the security operative hold all the aces if we do our job properly and continue with a workforce engagement mindset promoting that all important security culture. Structural building security will follow the principles of CP-TED and the onion skin/4D's principle. The building facade provides the outer perimeter of the building itself for our purposes. Windows and glazing may require, depending on your organisation, explosives or vehicle mitigation or general anti-theft reinforcements. Again, these will be clearly analysed and mitigated in your AI. As with perimeter security your building entrance(s) will be your most vulnerable point(s.) This will be dealt with in the next chapter.

Person Search

When people such as employees, contractors, delivery personnel or visitors enter/leave your building, or a sensitive area of it, you may require them to be searched. Searching your subject within your building is best done in a designated area i.e., behind a screen and via a hand-held metal detector with valuables placed in a tray and if required a bag search and/or pat-down. Effectively what you see at a high-profile sporting event when things are on high alert. The elements of it should be as follows and as your AI. They must always be same sex searches.

First explain to the subject the search requirement and process of the search (good practice means you will advise of a search process in advance as much as possible.) We are not the police, we are not looking for offences, we are concentrating on our security first and foremost unless there is a theft issue (however, this may well end up as just an internal matter if it is an employee.)

Take the subject into your designated area/behind screen and place valuables/metal items into a tray. Then conduct a search using both the handheld metal detection device (on vibrate mode) and a pat-down search over the main body areas i.e., chest, back, legs and arms. If you go onto YouTube, you will see variations of these to suit your own personal revision and practice.

Thank the subject for their cooperation, allow them to proceed and record interaction (as you have with vehicles.) As before with vehicles, do it this way every time and remember as:

> *Explain, area/screen - valuables/metals - device, pat-down – Record*

Basics of Building Security

Looking at the key basics of our building security we can also consider additional technical measures such as alarms and CCTV. But first let me concentrate your minds on the bricks and mortar side of things. By that I mean our walls, doors, locks, courtyards, internal parking areas, floor plan, basement, and roof areas and how you access them.

The operative must always remember two things regards their building:

- ☞ Know your building floor plan back to front and upside down. That is know it on paper and more importantly, walk it

- ☞ Anywhere in your building you can walk or have ready access, so unfortunately, can the rogue visitor/member of staff

Many of you will know your building(s) back to front already or if you have recently joined a new organisation you will be getting to know your building. But to be effective you must try to walk all areas of your building daily. If you have a large building you can zone it off and walk it, for example, over the course of a week. Here is why you need to do it. If you know your floorplan(s) when things go wrong, unexpectedly, your floor plan is already in your muscle memory and it will be easier for you to react without much thinking. Also know what type of walls and doors you have in each area of your building, i.e., are they penetrable such as a flimsy door or a plasterboard wall. So, you know the bad guy can force his way through a certain door or wall or, importantly, in an emergency can you force yourself and employees through as a means of escape.

As you walk your building(s) daily or weekly, you will see things you might not otherwise see, i.e., individual access card pads that may not be functioning at 100%, door locks that may be worn out or your key not turning properly or an unalarmed door left agar by staff, a minor flooding issue or faulty lighting meaning little used corridors or rooms/cupboards go untreated or everyone just assumes someone else is dealing with it. The motivated operative however will walk these areas and notice these things and report them accordingly. These walks may be considered patrols, but I know from experience that the little used corridor or room/cupboard goes unloved until there is a problem that is discovered too late. By knowing your floor plan(s) well and doing these little considered walks as your own personal security remit you cover three angles; you keep your memory fresh of your floor plan, you discover the little things no one else will and the odd employee that you will see in these areas now knows you walk them and why and the word will soon spread.

Essentials: Building

- **Building security should be based on the principles of CP-TED**

- **Layers should be implemented from within your actual building fabric complimenting the onion skin and 4D's framework**

- **Building security will always be based on Health and Safety, your AI, and a proper organisational culture**

- **Search people the same way, every time**

- **Know your floor plan well and that where you can walk with ready access so can the rogue visitor/member of staff**

- **Walk your floor plan on a daily or weekly basis keeping it fresh, making discoveries and spreading the word**

Security Lighting

This section will be short, as there is very little daily application for the security operative to be concerned about. However, security lighting is important and is essential to compliment your other security measures and it is worth knowing the key knowledge and practicalities. This is so you can complete visual checks of equipment and report things that might be an issue, without having to be an electrician.

There are several terms used as regards lighting fixtures and what they are supposed to do and not do, so in the spirit of this book I will give you the essential terminology and daily applications undertaken by the operative. Security lighting supports the principles of CP-TED and helps in other ways such as reducing the fear of crime. It can be subject to guidelines and regulations; it certainly is in the UK and comes under rules from local authorities and the Centre for the Protection of National Infrastructure (CPNI.)

Key Requirements of Security Lighting

☞ It must not cause a hazard i.e., to road, rail, or air travel

☞ It must not cause light pollution i.e., to the local community living near your facility

☞ It must not disadvantage security operatives i.e., when on patrol

☞ Installation must factor in inclement weather conditions locally

☞ Installation must avoid obstructions i.e., trees/overhead cables or avoid creating a new obstruction by its existence

☞ They must form part of your organisations AI

Basics of Security Lighting

Here are some basic terms that describe light itself and light bulbs/fittings and are useful to know. I have indeed described these in very basic terms:

☞ Lamp - i.e., light bulb means the inner parts and outer bulb case

☞ Luminaire - i.e., light fixture/fitting means the lamp and what it is attached to in terms of its housing and stand

☞ Lumen - total light output from a light source i.e., light bulb

☞ Luminosity - the perceived brightness of a light source

☞ Illuminance - i.e., light level that falls on an area of any given surface

☞ Colour Rendering Index (CRI) important for when using CCTV systems. Because it is concerned with the ability of a light source to reproduce the colours of various objects (scale 1-100.) So basically, if the colour of objects on your CCTV at night is blurry/too bright, then you need to change your offending bulb(s)

Purposes of Security Lighting

The three main purposes of security lighting are to support Health and Safety requirements, assist you in all your security operations in the hours of darkness and to provide the illumination needed for your CCTV. The key areas of any facility to require lighting will be the perimeter, the building(s) fabric, critical asset(s) areas whether in a building or specific area of the facility, ACP's both perimeter/building(s) and car parks. To achieve this the following lighting systems can be used:

☞ Perimeter Lighting - will generally be mounted on columns sufficiently inside to avoid climbers and will illuminate the perimeter fence/wall etc. and just outside it for CCTV purposes. But as already stated in the perimeter section not immediately on the inside of the fence/wall

☞ Building Lighting - refers to the targeted illumination applied to the vertical exterior of buildings. Allows for the intruder to be seen as well as any objects deposited

☞ Critical Asset(s) Lighting - refers to displacement lighting whereby much higher illumination levels are focussed on assets to move intruders away to other areas

☞ ACP's and Car Parks - will generally be covered by flood lights which light the entire area and are always in use

☞ As previously mentioned, the security operative must be aware of certain practical things on a day-to-day basis with regards security lighting, as follows:

☞ Make sure your emergency power generator is operative

☞ Be aware of all strike/off times of all relevant lights on your facility

☞ That your lighting is providing the correct rendition for all your CCTV

☞ Report any faulty/blown lamps

☞ Check on your patrols any damage to Luminaires i.e., columns

☞ Generally, on your patrols, check that all lighting systems are doing their job in terms of illumination

Essentials: Lighting

- Security lighting is an essential compliment to your other security measures and CP-TED

- Installation must avoid creating any travel hazards or light pollution to the local community

- Three key terms in security lighting are: Luminaire, Illuminance and Colour Rendering Index - remember these if nothing else

- Three key purposes of security lighting are Health and Safety, facilitating all your night-time operations and light for your site CCTV

- When on night-time patrols/CCTV operation always check your Luminaires, Illuminance, and the quality of your CCTV colour rendition

CHAPTER 4

Automated Entry Control Systems, Internal Alarms and Patrols

Supplementary technical security is imperative for your facility, it fine tunes your measures and protects specific assets. The main areas for these outside of CCTV will be access control, internal alarms, and security patrols. They again adhere to the principles of the onion skin and 4D's principle. What access control, internal alarms and patrols you conduct are facility specific and within your AI.

Automated Entry Control Systems

Closely linked to perimeter and building security, it is a key aspect of your first line of defence against unauthorised access of employees and site visitors. Referred to as Automated Entry Control Systems (AECS), it is a balance between hardware (i.e., doors, barriers) + software (i.e., cards) vs people + procedures. For unregistered users, the system should facilitate their identity (including photo), purpose of visit and with what employee.

The core objectives of any AECS should be to configure and recognise known users and to verify their authority to enter a particular location at any given time. It will also assist in the prevention of theft or items brought on site to facilitate protest or terrorist activity. There are various types of end user access as follows:

☞ Simple pin or passcode

☞ Actual swipe card

☞ Biometric requirement i.e., fingerprint

☞ Pin/passcode + swipe card

☞ Pin/passcode + swipe card + biometric

☞ Two person pin/passcode + swipe cards + biometrics (movie style)

In relation to access control management systems, as a standalone system, there are as always pros and cons. For example, as a comparison doors and locks. These always stay secure unless security is asked to unlock a door for which only they have the keys. Or someone opens a door that is secured by a locking magnetic system, i.e., not accessible even by swipe card but can sometimes be forced. These doors however are normally alarmed and/or covered by CCTV but not always, so require extra vigilance and monitoring by security.

There are four main areas of AECS, which will of course be used alone or in conjunction with other hardware or CCTV. On the perimeter at ACP's where employees may or may not (depending on authorisation) have access via a vehicle barrier. At the building gate/door

ACP's where employees will normally have full access. At the facility reception where security is located, but to help ease congestion at rush hour times, facilitated by card access speed gates. Internal doors throughout the building depending on authorisation and specific sensitive areas where for example valuable assets are located. This will obviously be strictly limited access and may include access only biometrically.

AECS daily

On a day to day basis how should we, as security operatives, be using and complimenting this widely used and excellent security system, and what are the pros and cons (in no particular order):

☞ You should monitor the system like you monitor CCTV, but obviously not as rigidly. That way you can see who is moving through a door at any given time and you get to recognise patterns of movement from certain employees. Particularly useful if they work in sensitive/asset rich areas of your facility

☞ You can use it to track people's movements where no CCTV is available

☞ Some employees (and normally the same offenders) have an annoying habit of letting other employees use their access card temporarily for convenience. By intermittent monitoring and use of CCTV see when this is happening and ascertain the other employee involved then make a written record

☞ If you are a new security operative at a facility you can use the system in conjunction with your CCTV to get to know employees quicker from a security perspective. By putting a name to a face

☞ It is an effective system when an access card is lost, and the employees' card can be blocked instantly

☞ It provides different levels of access over various time frames for example operatives will have access to all areas during all times. A standard employee particular areas between 9-5

☞ It is particularly useful for printed data tracking movements that may be used in any subsequent internal investigation

☞ System data may be extremely useful for any investigations by the authorities

☞ It can be effective in that it allows employees access via various doors (including pin/biometric) without the need to call security/need keys for locks etc.

☞ It can be ineffective in that it allows unauthorised people to tailgate who are not then challenged. Also, someone can 'catch' a door with the employee in front unaware of what has just happened

☞ Often stops unauthorised persons from getting through more than one door

☞ It can be disabled from doors and in zones to facilitate emergency evacuation

Essentials: AECS

➤ **AECS is a balance between Hardware + Software vs People + Procedures**

➤ **It can be made up of pin/passcode and/or swipe card and/or biometrics**

➤ **It can cover perimeter ACP's, building ACP's, reception speed gates/turnstiles, all internal doors and asset sensitive areas**

➤ **It is a valuable tool if used in conjunction with CCTV**

➤ **Remember the pros and cons of AECS**

Internal Alarms

This segment will be short but give you all the basics. Alarm systems are for the professionals and a vast area of detail, much the same as CCTV systems and security surveys. I will be consistent in steering you away from all that. However, the basics concerning alarms are very useful and the operative needs to know about them. It is not just for the security manager and the alarm company to be concerned with. Generally, alarm systems are made up of control panel units for all your alarms, sensors/detectors and alerting devices which you can hear both at the control panel and the location itself, but not always at the location so not to alert the bad guy, whilst you send other security to the location. The type, quantity and level of alarms at your facility will be site specific and subject to AI.

Key Alarm Systems

There are two key systems both with panels which will no doubt be connected to the security control room:

1. Fire alarm systems

2. Intrusion Detection (burglary) alarm

Fire alarm systems are the most important alarm system anyone can ever have simply because they save lives. There is also a legal and insurance requirement. They are normally operated from a panel and are in zones on that panel, from where the alarm can be identified and thus controlled and from where you can instantly decide how to best evacuate your building. Smoke or carbon monoxide detectors trigger the alarm, and some will activate sprinklers and/or close fire doors.

Intrusion detection alarms are the most advanced of the entry alarm systems, come in many formats and can be very expensive. They will undoubtedly be managed by the security control room at your facility, where the operative sits and controls everything that goes on around the system. These systems in a larger facility will have some or several integrated different types of alarms which make up the system as follows:

☞ Motion sensor alarm - uses optical (visual), microwave/infrared (heat) and acoustic (sound) technologies to detect movement. A classic and well used alarm

☞ Door alarm - these come in two types; first, door-forced-open alarms activate when exactly this happens i.e., a door that needs a swipe card is physically forced open. A tactic used frequently by thieves in corporate buildings where there are lots of thin glass doors. Second, door-open alarms whereby the door is opened for example by swipe card and then held open for a certain amount of time i.e., a thief tailgates and then props open the door to facilitate a theft. Or as is generally the case, the door is legitimately opened by an employee who props it open or is busy having a chat with another employee whilst holding the door open, this happens a lot. Door alarms can operate with a magnetic strip on the door panel and a sensor on the door frame. Disrupted contact between the two (sometimes on a timer) activates the alarm

☞ Glass break/shaker alarms - an alarm fitted to a window/door/standalone glass construction that is activated if a pane of glass is shattered or broken. More sophisticated shaker alarms may use a microphone or other element which monitors noise or vibrations coming from the glass unit i.e., a museum case. If the vibrations exceed a certain threshold (that is sometimes selectable) the alarm will be activated. As with all these alarms performance and sensitivity are mostly reliant on quality and cost

Internal Alarms daily

From our practical perspective, there are some things we should know and do in relation to alarms and alarm systems. First, we should familiarise ourselves with any important alarm panel system and the numbered zones in which it operates, be it fire or security. Walk those zones and know their number and colour coding on the panel(s.) That way if you are not in the control room and on a patrol and hear an alarm you can immediately confirm your location and zone for other operatives in control/on patrol and can assist in any evacuation. Again, this is being efficient and knowledgeable.

When on patrol and as a contrast to your knowledge of the panels, get to know three things about your alarm units/sensors (much the same as your CCTV cameras):

☞ Where the main ones are in the building or sensitive asset rich areas

☞ What the alarm/sensors look like because sometimes, for cost reasons, unit/sensors can change design over time. Also, some alarms/sensors may be near others with a different purpose i.e., shaker alarms

☞ Visually check (this can still be done from a distance) if there is any damage to an alarm i.e., part of the casing has fallen off or any wires protruding or hanging down loose

Essentials: Internal Alarms

- **Generally alarms are made up of alarm control panels, sensors/detectors, and alerting (sound) devices**

- **Fire alarms systems are by far the most important as they save lives**

- **The main integrated security alarms are motion, door, and glass/shock**

- **Know where your alarms are, what they look like, visually check them**

Patrols

Patrols are carried out essentially to provide a visual deterrent and to proactively identify or react to breaches of security. The time, types and frequency of patrols will be dictated by your AI and should be part of a daily shift briefing and be planned patrols i.e., where you have vulnerabilities or have had recent problems, to maximise effectiveness. Patrols may be on foot, in vehicles, alone or in pairs.

Types of Patrol

The four main types of patrol are:

1. First or initial patrols - done to deal with any issues left from overnight

2. Random or routine patrols - made either infrequently or at set times. Preferably patrols will always be random to prevent the bad guys being

able to predict when there will be a security presence. If your I.A.'s indicate a static presence is required at a facility location(s) most of the day this will more than likely be at reception areas, where you have sensitive asset(s) or when you are low on staff to help maximise the visibility of security personnel. A well-known police tactic so that many more staff/visitors see you and thus security numbers seem higher

3. Snap patrols - immediate patrols may be required to deal with incidents, such as reports of intruders, alarm activations or suspicious activity

4. Final patrols - carried out at the end of a shift to ensure everything is in order and to confirm what needs to be communicated and handed over to the next shift

Briefings

Briefings and patrols go hand in hand. In my world you cannot do one without the other. The police and other emergency services certainly do not. These briefings need to take on a certain form to be useful for the security mission and the operative themselves. Firstly, they should happen daily with your supervisor or subject to a handover by one operative to another if a lone worker. They should be updated during the day or night subject to changing information. They should not contain more than five bullet points, because that maximum number will be remembered by operatives. They should be retained in a folder/drive and subject to data protection. I am not going into detail regarding briefings because everyone in the security world should know what these are. However, they should always contain up-to-date information even if repeated from a previous briefing because it is still relevant or an ongoing issue and have a maximum of five pieces of information and where relevant have photos/images.

Body Worn Video Cameras

The use of body worn video cameras (BWV) has become increasingly popular amongst law enforcement and security operatives. They are extremely useful devices because they can provide audio as well as visual footage of an incident, which CCTV systems cannot. If used correctly between a team of operatives many camera angles can be gained as well as a larger field of view (FOV) or close-up facial images of the suspect. But again, this requires training and practice.

Make sure you activate a body worn camera for every single incident you attend or suspicious behaviour you have/or think you have encountered. Not only will it assist you later, but it will help you fine tune your use of the camera, your angles and positioning. A key tip here - always provide an audio introduction as you attend an incident and then some closing comments on the situation when it is concluded. This will look and sound extremely professional when on playback to your management or the authorities.

Patrolling daily

Finally, when patrolling always apply the following simple criteria for you personally in addition to any tasks given to you by your supervisors and/or the required standard patrols:

- ☞ As I mentioned previously, always walk wherever the bad guy can walk

- ☞ As also mentioned previously, walk those corridors that no one else does

- ☞ When on foot patrol always walk slowly because you see more

- ☞ When patrolling, always continuously scan your environment and remember to look up and behind you occasionally. Up because you might spot that alarm sensor that is broken so you can report it, and behind you because you might see that tailgater behind the person behind you and you can then put in a challenge

- ☞ Patrol as per your problems highlighted in your briefing and collect any intelligence as necessary, whether suspicious activity, equipment/building damage or breaches

- ☞ Find your own strategic static locations if it helps you i.e., inside of your main entrance for maximum exposure to visitors if no proper reception. Or near a main stairway so you can instantly go up or down to respond to an incident. This will be specific to your own facility that you know well, but my point is always finding yourself a few strategic static locations to stand that compliments your patrols

Essentials: Patrols

- **Patrols should always be planned and based on the most current briefing**
- **Briefings should have no more than five bullets points of information**
- **Patrol types should be first, random, snap, and final**
- **Always walk slowly because you see more**
- **Always have your own set of strategic static locations**

CHAPTER 5

CCTV

The subject matter of CCTV equipment, its specification, legality and operational use is vast. So, in this chapter I will concentrate on the basics of these areas but not get involved too much in two things. First, the specification of any equipment from a technical perspective. Second, legislation as this will vary between the USA, Canada, the UK, and Europe. What I will touch on is best practice rather than anything in-depth in the legal field. That is for you and your organisation to adhere to under the laws of which your country currently operates. CCTV cameras were first used during World War II in Germany for the Nazis to observe rocket attacks on the UK. Their development then continued in the USA during the 1950's for use in the civilian medical field. Subsequent use of CCTV has been developed to a very high standard with high-definition cameras being used by governments, in warfare settings and for satellites and space exploration.

Key reasons for CCTV

There are three key reasons for CCTV:

1. To obtain visual information/evidence about any situation that is happening

2. To obtain visual information/evidence about any situation that has happened

3. To deter by its presence, criminal or suspicious behaviour and thus increase your security capacity immeasurably

CCTV Systems and Equipment

Most modern systems are now digital, making use of computer technology. The best (more expensive) systems will be integrated with some or all of your other security applications such as PIDS, internal alarms and AECS. Regardless, a basic CCTV system will consist of cameras, lens, monitors and a recording capability, specifically:

☞ Cameras - in the main these will be fixed, pan tilt and zoom (PTZ) or dome which normally has embedded PTZ

☞ Lens - wide lens, standard lens, and close-up lens. The wider the lens the greater the field of view (FOV)

☞ Monitors - with the system allowing for matrix/multiplexer options

☞ Recording System - digital with instant playback/hard drive storage

All cameras should be high definition, with some systems including infrared and/or motion activated cameras. However, the quality of any CCTV across your control room will always rely on the quality of the technology you are using and this invariably comes down to cost. There are several existing, new and emerging systems continually being improved or developed such as automated licence/number plate recognition (ANPR), behavioural or facial recognition which is real high end technology.

CCTV Regulation (UK)

In the UK CCTV systems must operate according to several different types of legislation and codes. Other countries have their own, so I will leave it with you to do your own research but remember to keep it simple.

To keep it simple for those of you working in the UK, the previously mentioned Data Protection Act 2018 provides the umbrella legislation for the Information Commissioner's CCTV Code of Practice. The Information Commissioner is the head of an associate UK government department that oversees all protected data issues, including CCTV images in the UK.

In terms of CCTV, for an image to become protected personal data it must show sufficient details to identify an individual i.e., a bigger size image with clarity and focus.

The DPA requires that all CCTV systems should be registered with the Information Commissioner's department. One of the main reasons for this is CCTV on the perimeter of a facility i.e., a CCTV camera that can see onto the street and highway. These cameras can therefore pick-up images of persons outside of your facility. Each system must also have a designated Data Controller i.e., the head of your security department or the company lawyer.

This department also facilitates/issues guidance on another code, the Freedom of Information (FOI) Act 2000, so that the public have certain rights to access information from public authority bodies only. That is all I will say relating to the Commissioner's department, DPA and FOI as regards CCTV.

Remember, as previously mentioned, you must always consider data protection in conjunction with human rights law and always work as per your own AI. Section 7.4 explains the most useful bits of the code, to submit to memory and to facilitate your own personal best practice (in no particular order.)

CCTV Key Codes of the Practice

- ☞ CCTV must always be for a specified purpose (security at your facility) which is needed for a legitimate aim (to maintain that security) and to meet a pressing need (i.e., an incident.)

- ☞ There must be transparency in the use of CCTV, including a published contact point for complaints and access to information.

☞ No more images and information should be stored than those required for the stated purpose of the CCTV and deleted when that purpose is fulfilled.

☞ Access to images and information, whether live or stored, should be restricted, and only authorised when the correct policy and procedures have been followed.

☞ Any CCTV which compares against a reference database for matching purposes i.e., AECS must be accurate and up to date.

☞ There must be a clear chain of responsibility and accountability for a CCTV system, its operation and collected images and data i.e., from the CCTV operator through to the data controller.

☞ There should be effective review and audit systems in place of CCTV use.

In addition to your organisation's CCTV requirements, it should be used in an effective way to support health and safety and law enforcement.

> *Purpose-Contact-Stored-Access-Matching-*
> *Accountability-Audit-Support*

CCTV Importance of Privacy

Operating CCTV assumes a great responsibility on your part and requires a clear understanding of privacy and that interpretation of privacy is ultimately down to common sense. That tells you that if it comes down to common sense nothing less than the correct use of CCTV is acceptable and it could end up with you in prison. There are different levels of privacy according to the circumstances at the time. Clearly CCTV cameras are never actually located in restrooms or changing rooms, and neither are they located to facilitate any kind of views into those areas. Now that may seem an obvious statement to make, but you will be surprised how many people inside and outside the security world do not know this.

There is an expectation of privacy which is placed on the CCTV operator depending on where the person on the CCTV is located. In a public place the expectation of privacy is lower as we are unlikely to be doing anything of a private nature. In a private place i.e., someone's backyard/garden, our expectation of privacy is high. It is all obvious stuff, so you see the operative has no excuses. This is an important and fundamental principle of all CCTV operational activity.

Crucial to this is the operation of targeting and tracking which is much more widely used on an individual or a vehicle. When operating CCTV in such a manner it will provide extensive images and information on persons and their movements in a particular area. It is therefore important to remember their human rights in relation to data protection and that certain targeting and tracking must be justifiable and proportionate i.e., if you look at certain people on CCTV for a lengthy period and in a certain way, such as a camera zoom, you might be committing a crime of voyeurism. Contrastingly, any justified target and track would more than likely involve a written log to accompany the images which would then be saved on the server, subject to supervisor review/disposal.

CCTV Gaining the best possible Images

Remember the goal of a CCTV operative is to gain the best possible images. This can be done by applying the follow procedures:

- ☞ Do not monitor CCTV longer than is allowed without the requisite break

- ☞ A single operator should not monitor more than 16 cameras at one time

- ☞ Reduce the number of screens when activity is detected or needs monitoring

- ☞ AI may dictate certain screens need constant monitoring and others are placed on a cycle

- ☞ Separate resolute (private facing) screens or preferably a separate room will be required to view images live or retrospectively. This will therefore enhance privacy and data protection i.e., an incident concerning law enforcement or an internal company investigation of a theft

For CCTV operatives to assist an investigator or for security intelligence gathering, it is always best practice to obtain a close-up image of persons or vehicles even if you suspect suspicious activity, but then your suspicions are not confirmed. It may transpire the best quality image you now need was a missed opportunity the first time around

The following is a UK national standard for the types of screen image required in relation to the committing of crime or suspicious behaviour/activity, which will meet an evidential threshold:

☞ Detect - the figure/suspect occupies 10% of the monitor, so refers to actual figure/suspect presence at the location

☞ Observe - between 25-30% allows for any distinctive descriptive details

☞ Recognise - 50% allows an operative to confirm if suspect known/seen before

☞ Identify - occupies 100% and allows for identification

☞ Inspect - at 400% resolution on head and shoulders to allow facial recognition of a target individual

Essentials

👉 **The three key reasons for CCTV are a situation is happening, has happened, is a visual deterrent**

👉 **Your sole purpose with CCTV is to provide the best possible images**

👉 **A CCTV image becomes protected personal data when it is big enough to identify an individual**

👉 **Remember the eight-word summary of the CCTV code**

- Privacy is a fundamental principles when you are a CCTV operator (or viewing previously recorded images)

- For identification purposes a suspect must occupy 100% of the monitor

CHAPTER 6

Security and Health

I decided to add this particular section considering recent 2020 events. Make no mistake UK figures last year showed that at the height of the COVID 19 pandemic security operatives were in the highest risk group along with taxicab drivers and care workers, which is extremely worrying for us as a profession. I use the word contagion because the danger for us is not just in COVID 19 but any virus. Our world is a people world, and we meet and interact with them constantly.

As extremely safety and security conscious professionals we must take the lead on this. Both for our own personal well-being and the required enforcement and reminders to others. The bottom line at present is that not enough people have been following the rules and we must not allow that to happen in our facilities. It is not just about us all having the vaccine, events have shown that we must adapt and change how we live our lives in the future. Do not be surprised to see people still wearing a face covering for example. An overarching definition would be:

Contagion = the communication of disease from one person or organism to another by close contact

I am not trying to replicate medical or government advice. But simply give you a section that you can refer to as a security operative so when you need to challenge certain behaviour, you know your virus information. I will cover; intro to pandemics, what is a virus, how our bodies respond, coronavirus and its treatment and protection from it.

A pandemic is best thought of as a massive epidemic but with a wide geographic extension. Pandemics are more likely if the virus is new. COVID 19 easily meets these criteria and even with a vaccine, containing the virus and reducing the 'R' number is vital. Pandemics cause significant economic, social, and political disruption and the likelihood of them occurring has increased over the last century primarily because of greater global travel and integration. A virus behaves differently from bacteria. Bacteria lives in and around us and some are useful whilst some are harmful. Viruses are microscopic particles and much smaller than bacteria. They replicate inside the cells of living organisms i.e., people, animals, and plants. They cannot survive outside of these organisms and will die off in a few days without its living (organism) life-support. Viruses cannot be killed by antibiotics and some viruses mutate (change) over time as we have seen recently with the COVID 19 variants. Therefore, specific antiviral (vaccine) medication may be required for each different strain of the virus.

There seems to be two ways that our bodies try to fight a virus. By expelling the infection, such as coughing, sneezing, or vomiting or by way of fever as your body increases its temperature to kill the virus or prevent it from replicating and both these tie in with two of the three main symptoms of COVID 19. Weaker immune systems are also important here, whilst adults in general have a strong immune system, certain groups are susceptible. The very young or the very old or people with existing illnesses will suffer more consequences.

What about Coronavirus generally? Here are some simple overarching facts that are worth knowing.

Coronaviruses are a large group of pathogenic (anything that can cause a disease) viruses and cause respiratory illness including:

- SARS - severe acute respiratory disease

- MERS - middle east respiratory syndrome

- Common Cold

The new strain causing COVID 19 is written/known as SARS-CoV-2

COVID 19 (Coronavirus Disease 2019) allegedly originated in Wuhan, China around December 2019. The source of the virus is believed to be related to the seafood and live animal market in the city. It is not a black Swan event. In terms of the black Swan events mentioned previously in the security risk section, the authorities and the World Health Organisation (WHO) were aware a new virus was imminent, it was a case of not if, but when, where and how.

COVID 19, the spreading of the virus, the symptoms, dangers, and protections. Here are some WHO facts:

- ☞ It is an airborne virus

- ☞ It is mainly spread by respiratory droplets via coughing or sneezing

- ☞ Indirect transfer occurs via a contaminated surface and then touching your mouth, nose, or eyes. However, transfer is primarily airborne.

- ☞ The spread is increased with large numbers of people in poorly ventilated areas

- ☞ The main symptoms are new continuous cough, fever, loss of taste/smell

- ☞ Symptoms of the virus range from mild to severe

- ☞ Those symptoms generally appear between 2-14 days

- ☞ Young people are likely to have no symptoms or very mild symptoms

- ☞ Most people, who are reasonably fit, can recover within 2 weeks. Hence a self-isolating period in the UK of at least 10 days at time of writing

- ☞ Older people over 70 or those with certain pre-existing conditions such as heart or lung disease or high blood pressure are extremely vulnerable

The protections we require are so simply and as security operatives we have a responsibility to make sure these are adhered to. Always be conscious of those around you even in your own security department and all those other employees you now see daily. Just watch daily how people flout the simple rules which are currently in effect and may remain in certain circumstances even after mass vaccination is complete and the 'R' number significantly reduced. You do not know how often people are washing their hands, but you know what you can see and how a person conducts themselves. So, you personally should aim for:

☞ Face Coverings always - even outside if an area is busy with people as a visual example and reminder to others

☞ Keeping your distance is key – always be aware of your immediate surroundings and remind employees of this when the need arises

☞ Keep your security areas clean and tidy, if you minimise the clutter around you and keep your basic equipment etc. clean, you minimise risk

CHAPTER 7

Security Investigations and Business Continuity

I have, in my formative years in security, seen that there is a distinct lack of knowledge when it comes to all aspects of basic investigation activity. This was an early realization for me having spent two decades in the police service coming into private security and feeling immediately that the security operative was missing a large slice of key knowledge. For me, that means people are missing out on skills and knowledge that can be interwoven perfectly with all other security activities...and I mean literally all of it.

At the forefront of any corporate security operations is a desire to manage risk, primarily ones that can shut down your business overnight. When that kind of risk takes shape in a threat, or has happened, some kind of investigation will always be required. Even if it is serious terrorism related issues, led by the authorities, we still want to conduct our own investigations. Not just for any incident, but for our future mitigation strategies.

Now if you work for a large organisation, I am sure your security management team will have everything in place or should. You will probably find that your security management team may undertake investigations, in the main on behalf of the Human Resources department, for some internal matter concerning an employee usually a theft or harassment incident. However, there is a large part of the security world that does not fall into the large corporation category and where investigations do not really fall with the security department. In my experience investigations are usually undertaken by HR department staff which they conduct, well, quite badly. This normally happens because they are more concerned with the company's reputation then concentrating on finding out the truth. Also, I have personally not come across anybody in a HR setting that knows much about investigating. For me, your organisation's senior management team or senior HR staff oversee an investigation and the security department, using both management and security operatives, should conduct it.

I will use the above comments as a starting point for this section. But what about security investigations and business continuity as a combination? Business continuity and crisis management are complementary activities. Business continuity follows the management of any crisis and with that comes a subsequent investigation for your organisation on what went wrong and how it can be avoided in the future. This may be what your organisation did or did not do pre-crisis, during the crisis or what it did in the initial business continuity period, or maybe all three.

Business continuity will be the senior of the two because it will be ongoing after crisis mode has been stabilized. These two areas are important to an organisation because the sole primary purpose of any organisation, regardless of its size or the service it provides, is the need to maintain constant operations. When an organisation is faced with a serious incident, it needs to respond effectively and be resilient in the face of adversity. For me, these serious and high-level subjects of crisis management and business continuity require investigative capabilities to complement their effectiveness. So, it figures if we can and should investigate these areas should we not investigate everything else within our organisation. Investigative know how also adds to our skills and knowledge in general and will make you as the security operative more inquisitive about all other areas of our security work, that from my own experience I can guarantee.

Essentials

- Most security operatives lack knowledge of basic investigation activity

- Management and/or HR seem to undertake most investigations in an organisation when they should not

- When faced with a crisis an organisation needs to respond effectively and be resilient

- Business Continuity and Crisis Management are crucial to any organisation so should be complemented with investigative activity

- Investigation in a security environment = better risk mitigation strategy overall and can

be interwoven perfectly with all other security activity and enhance the quality of those activities

CHAPTER 8

Planning an Investigation

Before dealing with the principal requirements of conducting investigations and presenting the findings we need a definition. My preferred simple definition of the process is:

> *The action of investigating someone or something via formal and systematic research and examination*

The primary duty of what I will call the Security Operative Investigator (SOI) is to secure evidence on behalf of those instructing them such as senior management or the HR department. That evidence must be secured impartially, legally, ethically, and then the integrity of that evidence secured, before reporting those findings and tendering any recommendations. It is always key to remain within the scope of the law or any other regulations, otherwise the SOI could find themselves subject to criminal charges by the authorities.

When conducting investigations, you will find that everyone always has their own version of events. But an SOI must always work on the basis that at times you will need to investigate other departmental areas of which you know nothing about so you need to accept that there may be a learning curve. But the advantage here is that you can look at things as an outsider to see what is or has gone on. All investigations require the SOI to be unbiased and without opinion about those they are dealing with.

Most importantly, remember these three key elements to investigation. First, within organisations most investigations will be concerned with employees at all levels and what they have allegedly done. This will more often involve a use or ongoing abuse of power i.e., a manager interacting with their staff or someone with unrestricted access to IT systems. Second, there will never be a situation about which you cannot make enquiries. Third, never discontinue any lines of enquiry until you are certain they are completely exhausted. If we always use the definition as our starting point our investigation will always have three distinct phases:

1. Planning

2. Evidence Gathering

3. Reporting

The planning stage will consist of objectives of the investigation, required investigative collaborations, conflicts of interest and any consequences for your organisation of an investigation. All, importantly, underpinned with a written plan of your investigation's parameters, enquiries to be conducted and how you will report your findings. The evidence gathering stage is just that. Here evidence is gathered in several ways primarily documentary, CCTV, interviews and possibly surveillance. The reporting stage will involve a file with an executive summary and final recommendations. A presentation to senior management can also be made in addition to your file in circumstances such as post a major incident.

Objectives of an Investigation

The objectives of an investigation will be your starting point. Once those objectives are confirmed you can then formulate a plan on how you will gather the evidence and report. This will mean a full discussion with your SMT and/or HR to scope your terms of reference and establish the actual feasibility of the investigation. As mentioned previously the SOI will in the main investigate breaches within your own organisation. After that it will be criminal matters both internal with employees and external with your standard thief. Then the more serious incidents such as crisis management or possibly suspicious activity such as hostile reconnaissance. There will be a later chapter case study that will concentrate on an incident within an organisation involving a member of staff.

The generic of any investigation, however small or basic, will be to confirm or negate an allegation that is being made, or information that alerts you to possible wrongdoing. From that we will always look to do two simple things:

1. Obtain evidence that an incident(s) has in fact occurred.

2. Confirm a criminal offence and/or breach of organisational policy has been committed.

The investigation purpose, generally, will involve one or more of the following:

1. Disciplinary - disputes between employees or breach of company policy

2. Theft - including fraud

3. Damage to property - mainly insurance related

4. Due diligence - Employee issues relating to their recruitment

5. Health and Safety

In relation to the feasibility of any SOI investigation concerning the above five purposes any constraints need to be discussed and made part of the plan. They may involve any one or more of the following: legal, ethical, financial, timescales, availability of one or more SOI's to conduct enquiries separate from their normal security duties, logistics and equipment.

Before conducting your investigation ascertain if it is legal. Sounds ridiculous – not if it's called protecting your organisation from the subject and/or their union or lawyer. Remember, when conducting any investigation within your organisation regardless of whether legislation applies to your private organisation or not, very best practice is to follow the legislation provided to public sector authorities such as the police. That way if the matter ends up in court you, as the SOI, can show you followed best practice by following the legislation just like the police would have. Just do not get bogged down in it. You will know if something is not right. Something as simple as not advising an employee to seek legal advice when you know you should, unless it is strictly a disciplinary issue not requiring that.

Similarly, look at the ethical side of things. If it concerns a disciplinary matter of an employee about to retire, would it be in your organisations best interests to pursue the matter? Or would you demand that person attend an interview at your office just a few weeks after they have come out of hospital after a medical procedure? How much an investigation will cost your organisation is another important consideration in terms of SOI overtime, expenses, equipment hire etc. Here timescales are particularly important. Primarily because in the legal world keeping someone under investigation for an unacceptable amount of time without good reason or concluding an investigation is known as 'abuse of process' and can cause some cases to be thrown out of court. Apply these principles to any investigation you start. Additionally, management must make sure that an SOI is available and has flexibility regarding his normal duties to investigate. This is because focus and continuity of thinking during an investigation is crucial to the SOI being able to make progress.

Collaboration in an Investigation

Any investigation always involves collaboration. Without it you will not get results. But it will always be obvious collaboration and make sure this means your suspect too. The types of collaboration needed will become obvious from your plan. For example, if it involves theft in transit from your organisation to another you will need to strike up a relationship with your opposite number in the other organisation. Obvious I know, but this could be an individual you have never dealt with before, because until now you had no need to. So, you need to build that relationship not only to secure evidence from them but because they may need to go to court at the conclusion of your investigation if both organisations pursue a criminal court remedy.

The collaboration should take place within a vacuum of mutual respect and acknowledgment of the skill of your partners. With the appropriate sharing of information whilst accepting the limitations of any collaboration. The collaborations involved will include internal department and inter-departmental colleagues, external customers, company stakeholders, specialist investigators and consultants and public enforcement agencies.

Conflicts of Interest in an Investigation

If you do not deal with conflicts of interest at the earliest opportunity it will leave crumbs that the unions or lawyers will find later and use against you. Deal with them expeditiously, thoroughly and then record it. Conflicts of interest will be actual or potential, commercial, operational, ethical, legal and/or regulatory. For example, you are investigating of an employee which requires CCTV to be downloaded. One of your security colleagues is available to download that CCTV but is best friends with the other employee and they meet up socially. This colleague must not form part of the investigation by downloading CCTV. In fact, best practice would deem that they would not be permitted to even view the images and this should all be recorded in your report. This may seem like I am stating the obvious but you will be surprised how simple conflicts of interest are not rooted out right at the beginning of an investigation.

Here is another example you would probably think was made up, but it is true. A British police force in recent years investigated a horse racing jockey for betting fraud. This force then appointed a senior investigating officer to head up the investigation. However, that person had recently indicated to the force he would be retiring and had then been offered a job within the racing industry. That person subsequently decided not to retire, and coincidentally, the racing investigation then began sometime after. That officer, despite the previous job offer was appointed as the investigation lead. When the case eventually came to court the defence highlighted this previous job offer and therefore implied an impartiality in the investigation could have taken place. Again, seems an obvious conflict of interest, but it was ignored and that was by police investigators.

There are options in dealing with conflicts of interest. First, always address it promptly and disclose it in your file. Identify and remove it or pass the investigation to another colleague or if necessary, an outside investigation agency if you for example work for a small organisation. The consequences of not removing and disclosing the conflict of interest would include reputational damage when conducting investigations in the future, along with financial loss if sued a loss of confidence if collaborating with business partners or ultimately the loss of the case at court.

Consequences of an Investigation

The consequences of an investigation can be both positive and negative. In simple terms if you conduct any type of investigation, big or small badly and do not cross the T's and dot the I's employees, customers, stakeholders and even the local police will never take you seriously again. However, do a watertight investigation every time with thorough reporting and those people will have confidence in you. More importantly, the subject(s) of any investigation will fear an investigation every time one takes place because they know how meticulous the SOI and the security department will be.

Always remember the consequences of an investigation to your organisation and the subject(s). This is so you can remember the bigger picture in your plan and give your organisation options not to begin an investigation if they so choose. For example, the organisation can proceed and stop and/or recoup a financial loss or increase confidence of customers. However, if the issue is subject to court proceedings the organisation may attract unwanted media attention even if it is the victim, albeit they must then explain this decision to stakeholders or business partners. Likewise, the subject(s) of the investigation for them could mean that an allegation is completely unfounded, or a resolution found with the organisation in a mutual fashion. Alternatively, an allegation may prove to be the loss of their employment, a prosecution and a criminal record or even a negative impact on their character if purely a disciplinary issue.

Investigation Plan

Once all the above factors have been considered and confirmed you need to assess the information and type(s) of evidence that is needed to meet your investigative objectives. At this point remember that the investigation will always involve the cycle of:

Plan - Gather Information - Report

This will operate as the general framework for an investigation but also at a micro level with any information or intelligence gained as the investigation proceeds. It will include the following, but this is not exhaustive: documentation, signed statements, CCTV, interviews, open-source research and internal and external customer databases all intelligence which we look to further develop. An example of a generic investigation plan framework would consider the following: Investigation objectives, collaborations, conflicts of interest, consequences, legal requirements, evidence required and/or available, interview, surveillance if required and reporting. Here is a simple incident to start us off:

Scenario: A departmental manager has approached your security manager with an allegation that a member of his staff, John Doe, is leaving work early but still claiming overtime. This was inadvertently brought to his attention by another colleague in a different department who saw him in a local bar on more than one occasion (from a distance), when Doe should have been in the office working. The manager thinks that this has been happening on more than those two occasions that Doe was seen at the bar.

Framework

☞ Objective: Ascertain if a disciplinary and/or criminal offence has been committed and are the relevant evidential sources available to investigate.

☞ Collaboration: Ascertain what evidence can be gained by the SOI and what evidence is needed from third parties.

☞ Conflicts of interest: As per those conditions previously mentioned.

☞ Consequences: For both the organisation and John Doe.

Next you will be looking for your actual evidence and then reporting. These two areas will be dealt with in the subsequent sections but for the purpose of this plan I will give you some basics now. To keep things simple though I will not deal with legal issues here, safe to say you will always have a number of these for any investigation that you must consider and factor in.

Evidence: statement from the department manager; payroll department statement and documentation showing overtime has been paid; statement from the colleague at the bar, but only if he is willing as reluctant witnesses generally are of no use; access card information to track movements of Doe out of your facility when he should have been working and also not having returned; CCTV showing Doe leaving the facility to compliment access information; Interview with Doe making sure he is given the option of a solicitor if the money concerned is great or a union representative or at the very least a colleague who acts as a 'friend' in the interview.

Doe: subsequently admits in interview leaving work early on those two occasions and on two other occasions. These four dates are confirmed by your previous access card information and CCTV enquiries and by payroll having processed the overtime on all four occasions.

Report: the investigation with a full file giving recommendations for actions by your organisation. In these circumstances and considering the actual amount of money received by Doe, the recommendations would include the following:

- ☞ Pass the file to police for a criminal prosecution (more on this later)

- ☞ Instant dismissal with money stolen deducted from final pay

- ☞ Final written warning with money paid back immediately or salary deduction(s) and Doe no longer permitted to undertake overtime for the duration of his employment.

Remember whatever action is taken it must always remain confidential and not disclosed to other employees other than the departmental manager involved, HR and senior management.

Essentials

- Remember the simple definition for an investigation and an operative should be referred to as an SOI when undertaking investigations so employees and alike are aware investigations are being done professionally

- You will investigate employees at all levels of an organisation and it will always involve a use of or ongoing abuse of power

- Before conducting your investigation ascertain if it is legal

- Decide if it is in the organisations interests to pursue any investigation

- Use the investigative cycle of Plan – Gather – Report

CHAPTER 9

Evidence Gathering

Legislation, Regulation and Company Policy

I have previously mentioned the importance of legislation, regulation and company policy in any investigation. There are several pieces of legislation and regulation used by public authorities. These should be used by the SOI because they are simply best practice. They will by their very nature enhance the quality of any investigation. The main pieces of legislation and regulation to be concerned with, excluding fire safety and health and safety (as these are large subject matters) are data protection, police procedures and criminal evidence, human rights, surveillance, laws relating primarily to theft and fraud offences and the use of CCTV. As I am based in the UK I will be referencing the law here, for readers overseas please refer to your own legislation and regulation in these areas, in the US this may vary from state to state.

This section contains quite a lot of information in the context of keeping things basic. However, legislation is important and cannot be too basic. I have taken key pieces of legislation and simplified them. Areas of company policy have also been highlighted as a useful reminder.

Data Protection

I have previously discussed the issues around data protection and investigations involve lots of data. So this legislation is best practice and key in any investigation from planning to reporting for the SOI, it is therefore worth repeating below the key aspects of that GDPR legislation:

☞ The processing of data must be lawful

☞ And for a specific purpose

☞ And then only data which is necessary

☞ This data new (or already stored but updated) must be accurate

☞ This data should be deleted when no longer required

☞ This data should be processed and stored in a secure way

☞ The designated data controller is accountable for all the above

So, as in your normal security activity commit the following line to memory. It is a key responsibility and will also involve monitoring and enforcement by your supervisor or line manager at various key stages of your investigation. The protection of data is key alongside evidence gathering and conducting interviews.

Lawful-Specific-Necessary-Accurate-Deleted-Secure-Accountable

Police Procedures and Criminal Evidence

This area of legislation is key in getting your investigations up to the standard of law enforcement and drawing clear lines on the responsibilities of all those involved in an investigation, however large or small their involvement. In the UK there are two key pieces of legislation that in the main currently cover this. The Police and Criminal Evidence Act 1984 and the Criminal Procedures and Investigations Act 1986. Of course, legislation will have been subject to amendment or will be in the future. That is fine for you as the investigator as you will always check your relevant legislation before any investigation. But remember to simplify what you read and check because during my years in the police and practically, what is produced at the end of an investigation is generally not complicated. Why? Because no one outside of lawyers generally understand it, most of all a jury at court if any of your evidence ever ends up there. So, use the legislation as your framework but do not spend hours and hours reading acts of legislation because there are no surprises in there and the minutiae will not actually help you. I will now break down the main elements of this legislation to use as your reference points.

The Criminal Procedures and Investigations Act effectively deals with the roles and responsibilities in an investigation and the disclosure of evidence, basically to the defendant and his lawyer at court or the company employee you are investigating. So the following needs to be facilitated:

☞ Whoever is placed in overall charge of an investigation i.e., the security manager receives the terms of reference from the SMT or HR and decides on their team

☞ They decide how many SOI's will be attached to an investigation

☞ Decide the actual roles and responsibilities of each SOI. For example, one deals with statement taking, one deals with CCTV, one deals with the interviews, one deals with the security, integrity and continuity of all evidence and its written record. It may be that depending on the size and timescale of an investigation, one SOI may do all of this or maybe two or three SOI's at most. This is for the planning stage, but it must be flexible

☞ Disclosure of evidence is particularly important in an investigation. This does not mean disclosure of evidence to people not involved in the investigation such as the SMT members as they get a final report (remember data protection.) But rather advising your suspect employee, their lawyer, union representative or work friend what the allegations are and what evidence you have i.e., statements, CCTV, access card data etc. In my experience, as most investigations within an organisation will not be complicated there is no need to with-hold information to catch people out. Simply disclose what you have because they will either admit wrong-doing or they will not. They will only lie

during an interview if your evidence is not watertight or they see an opportunity to keep quiet on a
particular issue if your evidence is not conclusive
enough

☞ Disclosure also means keeping every piece of
information you come across, even if it is not
contained in your final report. It must be retained
separately and securely and made available for any
scrutiny this is known as Undisclosed Material,
more on that later. I will repeat again this is your
framework legislation for organizing your
investigation team and their individual
responsibilities and disclosure. It is also a must for
showing everyone else you use best practice just
like public authorities in organising your team and
managing information

Police and Criminal Evidence Act – Codes of Practice

This is the key legislation used by the police in England
and Wales (Scotland have their own which I will not be
referring to.) It is known by the police as PACE. To simplify
it I will divide it into its five sections and give you the brief
explanation that you need:

1. Searching – person and premises (codes A and B)

2. Arrest – (code G)

3. Custody – (code C)

4. Interview - of suspects (code E)

5. Identification – of suspects (code D)

For me to go into any detail about any of these sections will be to go against the premise of this book, but it is well worth investing in a copy of this book from a legal bookshop or Amazon, make sure it is up to date. Do not use the internet as a source of current legislation, unless the government website, have a hard copy of this PACE book and use it like the police do, as their Bible.

PACE in Brief

Searching

In an investigation you will not have powers as a civilian to search people or premises. When mentioning people, we are also referring to property under their control such as items in their vehicles that are parked on your facility, in their desks and their lockers. This can only be done if it is a condition of their employment that employees will be subject to searches of the person and their vehicles as they leave the facility (much the same as done in the motor car industry) or their desks/lockers if they are on site and an allegation has been made. An authorized person i.e., security or manager can then conduct a search with the employee present. This must be done sensitively and confidentially.

Arrest

Bottom line. As a civilian SOI do not arrest people. Even if it is a UK citizen's arrest. This is not because the power is not there (further reading needed if you are interested), but because in terms of an investigation if an arrest is clearly required you should already have some basic evidence and report it to the police expeditiously and let them make the arrest. If an offence is obvious and just happened, such as a serious assault by one employee on another this is a real time incident and at this point not a matter for an SOI. Do not get bogged down with what are your powers of arrest in an investigation, this is for the police, you are evidence gathering primarily for your organisation and then for the police if the matter is passed to them for potential criminal charges.

Custody

I mentioned this section of PACE, so you know it exists, but it is of no relevance to your organisation, investigation or the civilian SOI. Once a person from your organisation is arrested by the police you will have no further contact with them unless you are called to court. If the person(s) involved contact you or another employee you advise the police. All your organisation needs to do is receive updates from the police, unless a member of staff is the victim and then they will receive the updates not the SOI and continue to supply the police with any further evidence they require. A point to note here is that if you have an employee who has been in custody and not arrived at work, unless it is a work-related issue it is of no concern for your organisation other than a normal absence issue. If it is work related and the matter is with the police at this point the person concerned will have been suspended on full pay, or they should have been.

Interviews

Interviewing will be subject to discussion later, but I will touch on some basics now. For the police interviews are always conducted under PACE and as an SOI you will do the same. It is concerned with all the procedural aspects of how interviews are conducted (not what questions you can ask) such as recording equipment that can be used, fitness of the person to be interviewed, their legal rights and entitlements, actual legal advice and representation.

Identification

Again, identification much the same as custody is of no real concern for the SOI as you can easily identify your own company employees, but I mention it here as it is an important aspect for the police whether they know for example, a repeat offender or not. This is because many criminal cases involve issues of identification and in the UK legal world there is a whole raft of legal talk around it. So just to add to your knowledge I will explain two key aspects of identification issues for the police so you are aware of it in relation to arrests made by the police and more relevant to our use of and their need for our CCTV. If you know and understand these two types of identification as an SOI, you will understand how police conduct identification when either CCTV is unavailable or the images from CCTV are not sufficient to identify a suspect.

First, if an offence takes place on the street or in a premises say a retail store and an identification of the suspect is made by the victim this is called a Street

Identification. It works, for example, in relation to an assault in the street where the suspect has left the scene, and the victim gives police a description of the suspect. This is then written down by officers and circulated over the police radios so that the description is logged, twice. The victim is then driven around the immediate location and the victim asked to point out the suspect if they see them, but not prompted by officers. If the suspect is seen by the victim, they point them out from the vehicle and the suspect can then be stopped and arrested. The suspect must not have already been detained by other officers (who might spot the suspect first) and an identification by the victim then made. In this scenario officers would just arrest the suspect and any victim identification would have to take place later. This method of identification is useful as the victim can see the suspect in real life and CCTV may not have captured the offence.

The second type of identification is the well-known Identification Parade. These days they are no longer a parade in the main. That is because it became difficult to muster even suitable people to attend a parade alongside a suspect and the cost to set these up was becoming too expensive logistically. It is done now in the main by using an identification parade of images on a computer screen. That way the police can retain numerous images of people (innocent of any crime just persons allowing police to use their image) to use alongside an image of the suspect. So, our victim unable to see the suspect on the street, was later made aware other officers had arrested the suspect based on the good quality description provided (a reasonable arrest by police based on a good description would be within a 20 minute window.) Police would then prepare for a computer-based identification for a later date where the image of the suspect would be placed alongside 11 others who look similar to the suspect and images that have been previously agreed by the suspect and their lawyer.

Rest assured this is the simplest explanation I can give you on computer identification. But is important for an SOI because if an offence occurs outside your perimeter fence if an identification cannot be done with CCTV images alone there must be an identification parade. Note, victims do not make an identification from CCTV images it must be done with a computer identification and contain eleven other similar facial images. I will not be revisiting the subject of identification again, but these are essential basics for whenever the police are using our CCTV to identify a suspect.

Human Rights Act 1998

Human rights in relation to the European Union and the UK needs to be considered as the first and primary overarching piece of legislation by the SOI as I have mentioned previously. Much of the act is not relevant to an SOI but there are two parts that are considered best practice when investigating. The act applies to public authorities and complies with the Articles of the European Convention on Human Rights and is expected to be retained regardless of Brexit. For law enforcement and thus SOI best practice they are Article 6 Right to a Fair Trial and Article 8 Right to Respect for Private Life and Family Life. In practical terms (especially if any investigation involves any form of surveillance by the SOI) I have adapted the two articles as follows to use as a foundation for your planning and investigation:

Article 6 – Right to a Fair Trial

- ☞ Entitled to a fair hearing in a reasonable time (due process)

- ☞ To be informed promptly of the nature and type of allegation against them

- ☞ To have adequate time for the preparation of their defence

- ☞ To have legal assistance of their own choosing (lawyer, union, friend/colleague)

Article 8 – Right to Respect for Family Life and Private Life

Everyone has a right to respect for their family and private life and their correspondence (so for example you should not be opening or intercepting their mail at work)

There shall be no interference with the exercise of this right except if in the interests of national security, public safety, the economic well-being of the country, the prevention of disorder or crime, the protection of health or morals or for the protection of the rights and freedoms of others. For most of these you would clearly already be calling the police. These two articles are very relevant if you wish to undertake surveillance of some kind in your facility such as keystroke logging, covert cameras or a listening device placed in an office or even recording a conversation covertly on your mobile phone.

Regulation of Investigatory Powers Act 2000 (RIPA)

This legislation will go together with the above articles and the act is key if your investigation requires any form of surveillance inside your facility. But there are rules and I will simplify these from a private/corporate perspective. Please note:

☞ Any statutory body must comply with RIPA guidelines if they wish to undertake any covert surveillance and use any related equipment.

☞ As an SOI the rules are more lenient. But when deploying surveillance and equipment you are expected to respect the reasonable privacy of any individual (or innocent third-party individual) that is involved in any recording or tracking and abide by statutory regulations on data protection. A failure to do so could result in prosecution. You have been warned.

RIPA does not just cover surveillance by police but also by other law enforcement bodies e.g., the Serious Fraud Office or the Serious Organised Crime Agency, the security and intelligence services MI5 MI6 and GCHQ as well as many other public bodies, including local government. The Act distinguishes between (Part 1) the interception of private communications and communications data and (Part 2) directed surveillance, intrusive surveillance and the conduct and use of covert human intelligence sources (CHIS) i.e., informants used by public authorities primarily law enforcement agencies. Here are the key aspects simplified excluding CHIS as these would only be used by public authorities:

- ☞ Interception of private communication (phone calls, emails, text messages, etc) are the most sensitive kind of surveillance

- ☞ Communications data is different from interception in that it is information about a communication rather than its contents (phone number, email address)

- ☞ Directed surveillance is surveillance that is conducted as part of a specific investigation and carried out in a manner likely to result in obtaining private information about a person i.e., following your suspect down a street

- ☞ Intrusive surveillance is surveillance that involves either a residential premises, a private vehicle, or using any kind of surveillance device. So, for example, planting a camera or listening device in a private residence

From the perspective of your investigation as an SOI and civilian/corporate entity as opposed to a statutory body, here is where you stand until any amendments to current UK legislation:

Covert Camera

You may use during an investigation a hidden camera(s) in the workplace to monitor employees. In any type of covert surveillance footage should only be used for the purpose for which it has been taken, which must be a legitimate security reason such as continuous theft. Remember, do not deploy covert cameras in areas where individuals would have an expectation of privacy, such as bathrooms, changing rooms and locker rooms.

Listening Devices

You may during an investigation use a device to listen or record people in public areas i.e., outside your building entrance or place a listening or recording device in an office or business area on your facility. It should only be used for the purpose for which it has been taken, which must be a legitimate security reason. Do not place a listening or recording device that will intrude on the reasonable expectation of privacy of an individual, i.e., in someone's car (parked on your facility that may be unlocked) to which you do not have permitted access, or in a private area such as a bathroom.

Phone Monitoring

This area is tricky and there are laws on recording conversations (further reading needed if you are interested but keep it simple), that should be strictly followed to avoid moving into illegal territory. Businesses can record phone calls between employees and customers for commercial performance and security purposes. However, use of the call telephone transcripts as evidence in your investigation should only be used when both people were aware that they were being recorded. So, in relation to your investigation any wrongdoing by an employee would not really involve them using phones they know are being recorded because they would no doubt use their own mobile phone. Regardless, your covert listening device would still be of evidential use to you even if it can only overhear one side of a telephone conversation.

Computer Monitoring and Data Collection

Computer monitoring and data collection has long been used successfully by governments and businesses monitoring internet use by employees for safe use of the internet. In relation to monitoring or data collection for an investigation there is much scope for the SOI. Your organisation must be the owner of the computer being monitored. You must consider privacy laws and must not breach any reasonable expectation of privacy of the employee whose computer is being monitored, even when it is without their knowledge. You can use, for example, keystroke technology to log employee internet usage and collect computer data for security reasons as needed for a legitimate SOI investigation.

Vehicle Trackers

Very useful if your organisation has valuable assets in transit and/or monitoring the use of company vehicles to produce data for an investigation or track movements of an employee. It is not illegal to place a tracking device on a private vehicle of an employee in certain circumstances, but you should always comply with privacy and human rights law. These covert trackers are generally placed underneath a vehicle. As an SOI and during an investigation you must deploy a tracker on a car in a way that does not contravene other legislation such as vehicle interference (such as placing it inside the vehicle.) You must also be in a public space or a space where you have implied private access such as your employee car park and not in the driveway of the home of the person being tracked. Then to collect the trackers personal data that can be used to identify an individual as defined under data protection law, requires the collector to be registered with the Information Commissioners Office (as you would be anyway working for your organisation as an SOI.) The use of the tracker must be used in a manner proportionate to the extent needed to gather information and cannot be achieved by other means such as physically following the vehicle.

To conclude, as an SOI during an investigation you can undertake all the above surveillance within the scope of the legislation using best practice. You are not bound by these rules if your organisation is not a statutory authority. However, you are still subject to the two human rights articles, data protection and expectations of privacy. This can be summarised as:

> *Human Rights – Data Protection – Privacy – RIPA*
> *– Statutory Authority?*

Theft and Fraud related offences

These are the classic offences that will be prevalent in a work environment that will come to court in some cases where the financial loss is high. I will not give you definitions here, as you will need to refer to criminal legislation at the beginning of any investigation to ascertain what offences you may have, if any. I will instead highlight three key points that you must keep in mind as they are sometimes overlooked by civilians.

First, the legal terms actus reus meaning the guilty act and mens rea meaning the guilty mind must both be present for an offence to have been committed. Remember the two elements - the act/the mind - as they are particularly important when you are interviewing suspects. This is because you will come across many circumstances in your investigations that will require a verbal admission by your suspect (employee) to bring it to a successful conclusion (but this still needs some form of corroboration such as CCTV or AECS data.) This is just how it is so just remember them when you are on the look-out for guilt at the start of your investigation planning.

Second, theft has a definition and its quite simple. But the key element in the definition is that a victim must be permanently deprived of their property for the offence to be complete. There is never any offence unless the circumstances of an act fit a legal definition. For example, an employee takes another employee's mobile phone home as high jinks, the phone is not used, tampered with or damaged and kept in exactly the same condition as when it was taken. That employee then brings the phone back to work two days later and the aggrieved employee angry, makes a complaint of theft. However, there is no theft as there was no intention to permanently deprive the owner of his phone. What you now have is two employees that might not be friends anymore and the wrongdoer given words of guidance by security or his supervisor.

The Fraud Act 2006 is a good piece of legislation because it is now very much a cover all for fraudulent activity. It may seem complicated in the legal books but just apply these three simple categories to any issue and any fraud will pan out:

- ☞ Fraud by false representation – the key offence and this would apply to your employee that submitted false overtime claims in the previous scenario

- ☞ Fraud by abuse of position – this could be the same scenario as above, but it is the line manager submitting his own false overtime forms. It would still be fraud by false representation, but fraud by abuse of position would also apply

- ☞ Fraud by failing to disclose information – this could be a new employee who has secured employment with your organisation but lied on their application form. They have therefore secured a gain for themselves with employment and pay and a loss for your organisation who would have never recruited them if they had not been lied to

Company Policy

Use this next section as quick reference material regarding what is generally covered in any company policy document. Company policy can be enforced by your organisation, disciplinary or otherwise, and help employers dealing with employee accountability, fair treatment and health and safety. Policies are also guidelines for legal and regulatory requirements, and any situation that could lead to serious consequences such as those that then require crisis management. Company policy also protects the business interests of an organisation and helps drive an organisations mission statement and what is expected by the organisation and its employees, as well as treatment of your visitors or customers. It will generally contain the following:

- Organisational – the company mission statement and what it means to be part of the company

- Health, safety, and fire – highlighting their importance and required adherence

- Equal Opportunity/Non-discrimination – because it's the law anyway

- Privacy and confidentiality – to protect the organisation its staff and customers

- Personnel – importantly for the SOI this will make generic reference to employee contracts which will then contain information about an individual's business hours, renumeration, benefits, holiday entitlement, sickness, and retirement

☞ Disciplinary – clarifies transgressions and thus can be used as a source document for the SOI when presenting their final report with recommendations. Policy will cover honesty and integrity, misconduct, technology use, unsafe behaviour, and poor performance (the last one not being an SOI issue)

Essentials: Legal

➤ **Always follow legislation, regulation and company policy as best practice**

➤ **Data protection rules can be remembered as Lawful-Specific-Necessary-Accurate-Deleted-Secure-Accountable**

➤ **As part of a team you will be allocated investigative responsibilities and make sure you always follow the rules of disclosure**

➤ **PACE is concerned with Searching, Arrest, Custody, Interviews and Identification**

➤ **In relation to surveillance always remember Human Rights – Data Protection – Privacy – RIPA – Statutory Authority?**

➤ **Always apply actus reus and mens rea and make sure an offence is complete by way of its definition**

Sources of Evidence, Analysis and Grading

Sources of evidence obtained by investigation and research must always be analysed and graded because it should always be considered primarily as intelligence that comes together to present a viewpoint. On this basis always work with an intelligence cycle of:

Collation – Evaluation – Dissemination

Any sources of information I give here is not an exhaustive list (and my own list) and will depend on the type of investigation you are involved in and where it takes you at different stages. Generally, sources of intelligence that become evidence will include:

- ☞ Statements – both victim and witness, these are key pieces of evidence. Never let these people write their own statements. The SOI writes the statements in the same way every time and make sure you write them so they are of a court standard. Make sure they have a legal declaration at the top stating that the statement is truthful and you end the statement confirming they are willing to attend court if required (if you foresee a criminal matter)

- ☞ Documentary – this is anything that is not a statement, CCTV, physical or an interview. They will end up being either an exhibit or stored away as undisclosed material. For example, computer printouts (such as access card information, payroll information, customer orders, stocktake sheets etc), photographs, video footage from a mobile phone, surveillance logs, incident book entry, company policy. These must have a reference number of the SOI who seized it

☞ CCTV – your digital images from the hard drive made into a copy on a disc

☞ Interview – of the suspect recorded on tape

☞ Surveillance – a source of information that will manifest itself into both statements and documentary from SOI's

☞ Physical – these in the main will become exhibits, such as a computer monitor stolen by an IT employee. Again, an SOI reference number when seized, is needed. Remember the above as:

Statements – Documentary – CCTV – Interview – Surveillance – Physical

As intelligence is collected the SOI needs to analyse and grade it before dissemination to others on the team that may have a responsibility for it, to use, further disseminate or store away. Analysis and grading will assist you in:

☞ Establishing patterns, links and the overall value of intelligence

☞ Assign a grade (value) to the intelligence gathered

☞ Look to corroborate all intelligence (if possible) to give it weight and reliability

☞ Re-visit investigation plan in the light of new information from the above three

Security and Integrity of Information

It is vital to maintain the continuity and integrity of intelligence and evidence in an investigation and ensure there are procedures in place from the beginning so that intelligence and evidence once 'seized' cannot be contaminated, damaged or tampered with. This is because the integrity of all your information is crucial not only for your own SOI credibility that your evidence is in no doubt, but so its use in legal proceedings is not jeopardised and it correctly informs the outcome(s) of your investigation.

To achieve this intelligence and evidence must first be securely stored, for example, by way of safes, locked cabinets and/or computer password/encryption, (and always have a back-up digital copy of everything by way of photocopy or photograph.) On collection of any intelligence or physical exhibits a chain of continuity must begin. This is best done by recording who obtained the evidence, when, where and from who, who on the team subsequently secured the evidence and who had or now has control and ongoing responsibility for it.

When information and evidence is then physically taken from secure storage or looked at digitally there must be a written log of who and when that item was looked at or opened for further scrutiny. If physical items are in evidence bags, they must be resealed and details on the bag(s) updated. If this does not happen every time, in my experience, the one time it does not is when you have a problem. To solve this problem on a team, allocate one person to be responsible for physical exhibits and that means you go to them every time to sign it out. They should be the SOI that is responsible for disclosure and they will also be the person that liaises with any law enforcement when handing over items that the police will then retain for court proceedings that may ultimately end up being shown in court. Remember as:

> *Storage – Continuity – Reseal – Record*

Interviews and Procedure, Security, Integrity

When conducting interviews as a corporate/civilian SOI make sure they are used only for suspects. Do not interview victims/witnesses on tape. All their evidence should be taken in statement form. That way you have a clear demarcation in your evidence and only suspects need their evidence recorded so it can be probed in a second interview if needed and because you will always supply a copy to them or their lawyer/union (more on that shortly.) Interviews on tape will always be formal, recorded and with legal rights and entitlements afforded to the suspect and always securely stored away. Suitable audio recording equipment (twin deck tape/disc) should be purchased and made available to an SOI by security management as well as a room suitably quiet and private.

On commencement of all audio recording (tape/disc) the following must be included in the introduction by the SOI to abide by PACE style rights and entitlements:

☞ That the interview is being recorded

☞ Time, date, and location of interview

☞ All person's present introduce themselves and describe their remit

☞ Confirm that the suspect is fit and well for interview

Advise that the interview can be stopped if the suspect wants to take advice from the person, they have with them or phone someone for that advice.

Advise the suspect that they will have a copy of the recording given to them in due course and use a seal on the one tape/disc that will be stored and never opened unless required at a disciplinary hearing.

In the SOI world the caution is not necessary, this is something for police interviews in criminal matters. The interview is being recorded and it would clearly be in the employee's interest to speak as opposed to making no comment for what in the main for you will be disciplinary investigations.

To achieve best interview standards you should initially use open questions and allow the suspect to speak before probing particular answers but do this in a chronological fashion. This following is an interview model called PEACE:

☞ Prepare (your plan for the interview)

☞ Explain (explaining the interview process to the suspect and their entitlements)

☞ Account (the interview itself)

☞ Closure (summarize any of your points, suspect has option of final comment)

☞ Evaluation (this is purely for you and deciding if second interview required)

Do not get too bogged down in the aspects of the PEACE model and the ins and outs of any particular evidence you have. Just go where the evidence takes you in interview and ask the relevant questions probing where necessary. In relation to any interview do not go all guns blazing trying to secure some sort of confession as the questions should supplement all your other evidence. The bottom line with interviews is you can ask all the questions in the world but there is only one that matters. Did you do it? Yes or No. I hope you take my point.

Continuity and integrity apply to your interview recording. Using a two-deck machine. One tape/disc chosen by the suspect will be sealed (simple protective seal) and details written on the tape/disc of start and finish time, date, location of interview and signed by the suspect and counter-signed by the SOI and any third-party present. Use the other tape/disc to make an additional copy for the suspect. Store the sealed copy away in a locked safe/cabinet not to be opened unless at a disciplinary hearing where there may be dispute over what has been said. For the sealed copy, an SOI reference number is needed for whoever conducts the interview. For example, the SOI initials/name of suspect/date: JL/Doe/21/12/19

Surveillance

Whenever you do this do it properly and follow the legislative guidelines. For planning, methods and equipment for surveillance use the following key points as your framework:

☞ Identify and locate subject(s), their vehicle(s), and their activities

☞ Choose the most appropriate, ethical and legal surveillance method(s)

☞ Identify what team and equipment is required and record that

☞ Check that equipment is working correctly and record that

☞ Allocate surveillance logs to those in the team requiring them

☞ Ensure those on any team know their role, do this by briefing

☞ Options for surveillance methods are single/team, electronic, static, foot or mobile surveillance

☞ Recon the subject's location so team members know their start position if static, foot or mobile surveillance

☞ Equipment that can legally be used by the SOI are mobile phone, radio, CCTV, binoculars, vehicle tracker, covert camera and audio listening device all in the context of RIPA and adherence to best practice

Crime Scenes

This will be short, but it is important because here you effectively need to do nothing. As a corporate SOI you will not be dealing with physical crime scene forensics, because you have no need too. If you ever need to seal off a crime scene that tells you it is a criminal matter and will end up with the police. Burglary is a classic example of a corporate crime whereby forensics are needed to corroborate other evidence such as CCTV.

So, if it is a criminal offence that has occurred that is clearly a matter for the police make sure you secure a crime scene on behalf of the police and thus secure any possible forensic evidence such as fingerprints/DNA. So in summary for a crime scene:

> *Do not touch anything – Secure scene as wide as possible – Guard it – Record*

Essentials: Evidence

- Sources of information gained for an investigation must always be analysed, graded and if possible corroborated

- Information/evidence will be statements, documentary, CCTV, interview, surveillance, physical

- Continuity and integrity of evidence will be storage, continuity, reseal, record

- Remember a suspect's rights and entitlements for any interview

- Remember the surveillance framework

- Crime Scene – simply seal it

CHAPTER 10

Reporting the Findings of an Investigation

The final part of an investigation is just as important as the planning and evidence gathering, tendering your report. I liken this to presenting a set of case papers to court in law enforcement and it should be of that standard. There can be more than one type of file presented but in my opinion you should only present one and that is a full file along with any physical exhibits. That way the timeline can be run through and the incident fully explained, but in a succinct fashion. In my experience one person writes and puts the actual file together in consultation with other team members, it is then reviewed and rubber stamped by security management.

Types of Report

If the investigation concerns for example, issues relating to a previous crisis management situation best practice would be to provide the organisation SMT with a presentation of your findings by way of a PowerPoint. As well as each SMT member being given what I call an abbreviated file with all the major points and issues highlighted to help them follow your presentation and ask questions. This method of presentation and file would be an excellent way of explaining why a crisis situation occurred, who may be responsible and how the organisation responded and what can be learnt and changed for the future.

Report Contents

Any file must still adhere to data protection and confidentiality and include the legislation and regulation used as guidance during the investigation and therefore highlighting best practice has been used to SMT members. The contents of a file would take on the following format:

- ☞ Front Cover – marked confidential with case reference number only

- ☞ Title Page – relevant heading, SOI name, date of production

- ☞ Contents – number of sections of file with page numbers

- ☞ Introduction – include the purpose of the file and terms of reference

- ☞ Executive Summary – why and how the investigation was conducted together why key findings and recommendations

- ☞ Investigation – a concise, clear, and accurate explanation of the whole investigation including timeline, methods used and reference to important documentary and physical exhibits

- ☞ Findings – of investigation and recommendations for action

- ☞ Appendix – including existence of any undisclosed material, exhibit reference numbers list, legislation and regulation and company policy used

Investigation Case Framework Example

I will use this section to provide a framework for an investigation that will require all the elements previously discussed before moving into the next section on business continuity. I will use the John Doe overtime scenario again but this time with the added element of surveillance measures. It will again be a disciplinary issue, with no police involvement and a report of your findings was produced. This will seem a very straightforward scenario and framework, however you will be surprised how many security operatives are not aware of these basics of investigation.

Scenario:

A departmental manager has approached your security manager with an allegation that a member of his staff, John Doe, is leaving work early but still claiming overtime. This was inadvertently brought to his attention by a colleague who saw him in a local bar on more than one occasion (from a distance) when Doe should have been in the office working. The manager thinks that this has been happening on more than those two occasions that Doe was seen at the bar. The manager also states that petty cash has gone missing from the office, and although several people in that particular office have combination lock cabinet access, there may be a shortfall on the days that Doe is supposedly undertaking his overtime and any cash request needs line manager authorisation and recording.

SOI Investigation Case Framework:

☞ Receive your terms of reference from security manager/HR/SMT

☞ Plan the investigation regards evidence required, legislation, team members

☞ Put in place confidentiality, continuity and integrity of evidence measures

☞ Obtain statements, documentary and CCTV without alerting Doe

☞ Install covert camera in vicinity of petty cash cabinet

☞ All information and evidence is now secured in relation to allegations made

☞ Doe is interviewed in presence of lawyer/union/friend (his choice)

☞ Doe is read statements, shown documentary evidence, CCTV, and surveillance footage of him accessing cabinet unauthorised

☞ Doe admits he is responsible (evidentially no other option)

☞ Report of findings submitted to HR/SMT with recommendations

☞ Doe has disciplinary hearing with lawyer/union rep with SOI present if there are any issues needing clarification

☞ HR/SMT make employment decision on Doe

CHAPTER 11

Crisis Management and Business Continuity

In the previous section on security investigation, I have simplified a subject matter that can be complicated for those not operating within law enforcement. The aim is always to assist you with simplified subject matter to help you practically on a day-to-day basis. In this part we will look at crisis management and business continuity. What it means in reality for the operative in terms of a situation that is generally above their pay grade and not within the realms of their decision making, short of providing an emergency logistical response. However, it is crucial you have a basic understanding of the mechanics of what happens during these events, what your SMT members should be doing and where you as the operative fit it to it all both during and after any crisis.

As with any security matter I prefer to use basic definitions that reflect the essence of the subject matter. Crisis management is always followed by business continuity activity and I recommend the following:

Crisis = any situation that has harmed people or property, seriously interrupted business activity or damaged reputation

> *Business Continuity = the capability of an organisation to operate at the same level prior to a serious incident (crisis)*

In my security experience unlike the emergency services, few corporate managers are really experienced in dealing with crisis management and business continuity because they never really get any input outside of medical situations and fire evacuations. Time spent on discussions, planning and most importantly training does not seem to be a priority for many organisations because it costs operational time and money and many organisations do not think that critical incident will happen to them. The bottom line is that your organisation can go down the pan long before your organisation realises that it does not have a plan to manage a crisis and neither does it have a plan to then maximise business continuity. The input I give you here will help you realise what the management should have been doing before, during and after it is all going wrong and most importantly what you can do as the operative that shows you did your bit within your remit and place in the organisation (and you knew what they should have been doing.)

Crisis management and business continuity has no secret formula, or one size fits all response that can be applied as the situations can be limitless. For example, environmental, employee, terrorism, political, breach of confidentiality by leak, malicious internet rumours that gather momentum, product defects and supply chain interruptions. A situation is not often detected until it is too late whereas if plans had been in place before or at least at the start of the process, the damage could have been prevented or at least minimised. Look at your organisation and its products and/or services and make discreet enquiries to see if crisis/continuity plans exist and are in place, along with your access to the plan and if there is any training that goes with it. You will be surprised.

In combining crisis management and business continuity it creates three distinct phases that your organisation needs to plan and act upon:

☞ Risk Analysis of Vulnerabilities and Continuity – their plan (hopefully a prevention one) and the subsequent business continuity phases

☞ Crisis Management – (them/us) in the immediate aftermath via containment

☞ Business Continuity – (them/us) speedy resumption of normal business activity

Crisis Prevention, Planning and Training

Types of crisis can be divided into three categories:

1. Patterns and Planning – a crisis incident occurs whereby a previous pattern of similar smaller issues where not acknowledged, linked and dealt with by senior management by way of resolution at the time or earmarked for future planning. For example, non-compliance by the same employees on safety issues

2. Slow Burn – a medium sized incident(s) but no critical damage. For example, large employee

unrest or political protest outside your facility that is peaceful and has not disrupted business activity

3. Sudden – the crisis has occurred and will get worse if plans are not activated immediately. For example, large flood and damage on site or significant injury to a number of employees due to accident

The planning and resources needed to prevent a crisis and undertake business continuity are far less than those required putting out a fire that is raging. To achieve this your organisation along with heads of department and the security manager should be conducting a risk analysis of all your vulnerabilities, in essence a full-scale health and safety and fire assessment in relation to both your general operational activity and external corporate communications. This would be done over a number of days brainstorming as well as periodic meetings so to fine tune things. The next stage is that your organisation should have written a crisis plan and most importantly, be communicated it to its employees so at a basic level they know it exists.

If your organisation has a plan and it has been completed properly it should manifest itself as a manual rather than a plan on just a few sheets of paper and it should contain amongst other things, specific to your organisational business the following:

☞ Contents – sections and numbered pages (that should be a given.)

☞ Introduction – along with mission statement, scope, policies and goals of the plan and why it is an important document for the organisation and its employees

☞ Core Crisis Team – who they are and what their responsibilities are. This will include key people from all areas such as SMT, security, operational, HR and corporate communications

☞ Crisis Management Room – your war room that will include staffing levels by the core team, its location and most important a communications infrastructure

☞ Response team(s) – who they are and what their responsibilities are. Will include a larger team of heads of department, who then allocate tasks to all members of staff under their control and any external specialists that are brought onto your facility

☞ Response Activity – what you will do as staff with any required flexibility

☞ Media spokesperson – a trained individual from whatever department who best imparts updates to employees internally and the external media outlets (including internet activity.) Also include pre-prepared generic holding statements on the specific situation. Any communication from them should be to you the staff first

☞ Business Continuity Phases and team(s) – covering actions over time (more on this later)

☞ Appendix of important documents relevant to your organisation

☞ Reference to the training that is needed to make the plan work operationally. A must have for all crisis management and business continuity employee activity

Now we have ascertained what your organisations hierarchy should be doing, all the security operatives can do is promptly and discreetly check these people are doing what they are supposed to be doing. The bottom line is crisis management and business continuity decision making may be above your pay grade, but they will still expect all employees to respond and help put things right during a crisis and after. You therefore in my opinion, also have a responsibility to point out any shortcomings in their planning (and write it down somewhere like an email to your security manager as a written record) for the better good. Not because the operative knows better. Below are some examples of what and how you can check your company manuals robustness.

☞ Is it based on the types of scenario that may affect your particular organisation

☞ Is it based on a thorough crisis/business continuity risk analysis

☞ Does it contain an overarching framework that highlights key management responsibilities and their requisite authority to make final decisions.

☞ Does it indicate a lead spokesperson and show pre-prepared statements for external media for various incidents

☞ Does it indicate the importance of communicating with staff in the first instance and on a regular basis

☞ Does it contain reference to staff training for a crisis incident and employee welfare and rest during the incident response itself

The production of a manual by your organisation for a crisis can be termed as a false economy if it comes with no practical training and therefore quickly descend into a logistical nightmare at crisis time. Training can be divided into training for the core crisis team, the media spokesperson and all staff training. It should include:

☞ The core crisis team should be regularly reviewing the manual in its minutiae from a practical perspective

☞ The spokesperson should be receiving regular media training and practice (use it or lose it principle)

☞ Most importantly, all staff should be receiving training in the manual itself with table-top exercises, drills focusing on particular group remits during a crisis and full-scale drills where everyone acts out a given scenario (use it or lose it)

☞ Any training should be properly de-briefed every time and necessary amendments made to the manual if it highlights deficiencies in the plan

Crisis Response

We know now what the management should be doing to prevent, plan for and train employees. Now although this is above your pay grade, and do not expect any invites to attend SMT training around the manual, you are still entitled especially as security to flagged up things you should be being told. The key two being how can I access the manual or at least a redacted version of and what training will I receive and how often, considering you are actually part of the security department.

Looking now at the actual response of an organisation to any given crisis this is where we see if the plan works, or how they work off-the-cuff if there is no plan. The crisis response will primarily be time sensitive in terms of the co-ordination of employees and other logistics.

At this point even as a security operative you will have no control or important decision making authority, you will effectively just do what you are told like any other member of staff (within your security remit.) The following needs to be activated by your core crisis team in relation to timescales - just so you know how they should be responding why you just do what your being told:

☞ Response Phase I (1-2 hours) – this will cover any immediate evacuation, emergency services call, staff mobilisation and attendance, increased and confirmed information gathering on the incident and activation of all aspects of that important crisis plan

☞ Response Phase II (2-24 hours) – this will cover anything ongoing by the emergency services, employee deployments both departmental and general to shore up your facility and save assets starting with those most critical. Interim liaison with staff updates first, then the first external media liaison with a pre-prepared relevant statement

☞ Stabilisation Phase (24-48 hours) – this will cover ongoing recovery work, ongoing media liaison which will be increasing in detail during this phase and start of the detailed damage assessment. At this point they should be looking to link in this phase in with business continuity plans

☞ Everything that has taken place during these three phases should have been logged and fed back into the core crisis team to assess and make any adjustments. The core crisis team should also update employees on the situation and how stabilisation is progressing and importantly check on current welfare of employees via their line managers.

Business Impact Analysis and Continuity Implementation

Before they set about implementing their business continuity plan which will, just so we are clear, be part of the crisis management manual a business impact assessment needs to be undertaken for the given incident. This is to best see how to implement business continuity in relation to all the information they now have, and the priority of your organisational needs. A business impact analysis I will describe as:

> *BIA = An assessment on the impact of the serious loss of assets and resources*

Primarily, key consideration must be given to the most critical areas of the business such as the most valuable assets then next how rapidly loses would have a detrimental effect on the overall organisation, and underpinning those two what employees, equipment and other resources are necessary to maintain critical business functions. The processes of this assessment would include:

- ☞ Listing the key products and services that have been disrupted that will have the greatest impact over various timescales, for example twenty-four hours, two days, one week and one month

- ☞ Identify maximum timescale that disruption can be tolerated before they become absolutely critical to the business

☞ Set a point in time when key products and services need to be resumed and should be convergent with the above maximum timescale

☞ List the activities and resources that are needed to meet the above set point in time and be able to resume normal (or as near to normal) business activities

Actual implementation of business continuity would be overseen by a team similar to the core crisis team, but not necessarily with the exact same members. Implementation would be a continuous and cyclical process overseeing products, services, assets, buildings and employees as follows:

☞ Employees – the most important part of any business continuity. It will have the correct number of staff to carry out critical activities, the correctly skilled staff for a particular task and a number of staff to help facilitate activities involving external suppliers or customers. You will be key here in co-ordinating this

☞ Facility and buildings – this will involve the use of the best available buildings and locations which in some cases may be external locations, which are fit for purpose. Particularly in terms of IT requirements, plant, machinery, security requirements and employee rest facilities

☞ IT and Data – will involve set up and running of critical IT and data systems for business continuity and consideration for the storing and protection of systems and data if for example, staff are now in a new location

☞ Suppliers and Partners – for example, priority now is given to critical suppliers and any additional tenders completed for replacement of or new critical suppliers. Also any new reciprocal arrangements with similar organisations that can assist you in critical services. For example, the loan of a large refrigerator trailer vehicle to help complete deliveries within the same business market (which will require goodwill from a competitor)

☞ Internal and External Threats – internal threats to be aware of could include, product problems, supplier problems, poorly judged media statements (even at this stage) or profit warnings. External threats could include unsteady economic market conditions already present in your sector, adverse weather conditions affecting the delivery of goods in addition to the incident you have already had and supply chain disruption that would have always been outside the control of your organisation causing a knock-on effect

Essentials

- **The three types of crisis are: patterns and planning, slow burn and sudden**

- **The planning and resources needed to prevent a crisis and undertake business continuity** requires your organisation to conduct a risk analysis of all their vulnerabilities in essence a full-scale health and safety and fire assessment in relation to both your general operational activity and external corporate communications

➥ This should manifest itself in a manual containing a framework for both crisis management and business continuity AND employee training

➥ As a security operative you have a responsibility to point out any shortcomings in their plan for the better good because during a crisis your input to SMT will be zero - because you will just be doing what your told

➥ Communication (which should always be on-going) to employees must be a priority for an organisation before any external corporate communication at each stage

➥ An immediate crisis response involves three phases: Recovery I (1-2 hrs), Recovery II (2-24 hrs), Stabilisation (24-48 hrs)

➥ An - at the coal face - business impact assessment is needed before business continuity plans can be mobilised

➥ Implementation of business continuity by a select team would be a continuous and cyclical process overseeing products, services, assets, buildings and most importantly employees

CHAPTER 12

Emergency Procedures

In this next section I will highlight emergency procedures in their different context. They will sit alongside crisis management and business continuity and practically still need investigating by an SOI or SOI team depending on the size and nature of the incident.

Standard Building Evacuation

Generally, unless you are security personnel or for example a fire warden, employees and visitors care very little about building evacuation and therein lies a simple solution for us. I will not discuss fire safety in depth here because it is a large subject matter and I am not qualified to do so. I will though draw your attention to some real basics, both admin and practically and again anything in this section refers to UK law and regulation (England and Wales.)

Your organisation is legally required to have a designated person responsible for fire safety management in all its aspects and would have received training commensurate with that. Under the Regulatory Reform (Fire Safety) Order 2005 that designated person must be competent and have carried out a full fire risk assessment (including periodic fire testing) for your facility, which must be documented. Employees must be provided with any relevant information, instruction and training (periodic fire drills) whilst working at your facility.

During a fire evacuation, or for something such as a power failure or flooding the process for employees is simple just leave the facility in an orderly fashion via the nearest designated exit, following the nearest safe signage for exiting the facility and as directed by security staff or fire wardens. Those procedures put in place by the designated person will then be followed. I say the process for employees is simple because you will be surprised how many of them do not just leave the building. Some sit in their offices until someone tells them to leave or others pussyfoot around in corridors and other office space not actually doing much leaving. So, when dealing with any employees when the bell rings no explanations, no conversations about post evacuation or how long it will go on for – please leave the facility immediately sir/madam.

Mail Handling

This will include letters, parcels, packages and anything delivered by post or courier. Suspect mail delivery items have been a tactic used by criminals and terrorists. Delivered items may be explosive, incendiary, contain sharps, blades or chemical, biological, or radiological (CBR) material. The term white powders are often used in the context of mail and encompass CBR as well as benign materials. Be aware that such materials may not be white and may not be powders. General indicators that a delivered item may be of concern include:

☞ Unexpected item, especially if hand delivered

☞ Labelling or excessive sealing that encourages opening at a particular end or in a particular way

☞ Item is addressed to the organisation or a title (rather than a specific individual)

☞ Unexpected or unusual origin (postmark and/or return address)

☞ More stamps than needed for size or weight of package

☞ Greasy or oily stains or odours emanating from the package

An explosive or incendiary indicator maybe where there is a heavy or uneven weight distribution within the package. CBR may include powders or liquids emanating from the package or stained packaging. Unexpected odours observed on opening and/or sudden obvious onset of irritation of skin, eyes and nose or feeling unwell. Your initial actions as the operative in this mail handling situation will be:

☞ If in doubt call the emergency services

☞ Do not attempt to open the item

☞ Place the item to one side so easily identifiable to emergency services

☞ Stop any further handling of the item

☞ Clear the area concerned and seal it off

Major Incidents

When the emergency services respond to a major incident, their initial response is crucial and time sensitive. What helps them to make that decision is the very first information they receive from either one of their own personnel or a member of the public who might be a security operative. Based on that information (in the UK) that is how they decide whether to declare something a major incident. If you have a number of casualties and need the full-scale attendance of police, fire and medical personnel you have a major incident.

When information is furnished to the emergency services whether by their own staff, public or security operative they will ask questions based on a mnemonic that gives them all the information they need. This is currently called METHANE and is a must know for the security operative and made up as follows:

M = Major incident declared

E = Exact location of incident

Confirm nearest street junction or exact address

Geographic size of the incident

T = Type of incident - Explosion, building collapse, firearms incident etc.

H = Hazards

Identify the hazards present or suspects such as number of terrorists/types of weapons being carried/used

Consider potential or secondary devices

Is evacuation or invacuation necessary and safe

A = Access Routes

Update with routes that are safe to use

Clarify routes which are blocked

N = Number of Casualties

List type and severity of injuries

Approximate number of presumed dead, injured, survivors and witnesses

E = Emergency Services required

State those emergency services required

Conduct a joint dynamic hazard assessment with the emergency services and full liaison upon their arrival

Make sure you have this Methane written down somewhere such as in the back of your security notebook, or on a laminated reminder card and do not leave home without it.

Suspicious Items and Stay Safe

As with major incidents this is key stuff to remember for the security operative and for me it goes hand-in-hand with your major incident mnemonic. With all suspicious items do not let those around become alarmed as to what you are checking out. Do you enquiries as quickly as possible to confirm whether or not the item exhibits the required suspicious characteristics, then apply the 5W's

1. What is it

2. Where is it

3. When informed

4. Who informed you

5. Why is it suspicious

If confirmed immediately start to apply the 3C's

1. Clear the area

2. Communicate to your security control room

3. Control the cordons

The Stay Safe principles are well advertised by the security services in the UK and tell the public three simple things to do during a serious life-threatening incident and the information that armed officers may need (especially from security operatives) in the event of a weapons or firearm attack.

Run – Hide – Tell

☞ Suspects – location, descriptions and direction of travel

☞ Further information - casualties, injuries, hostages and building dynamics

☞ Stop other people entering the building if safe to do

☞ Armed Police Response – follow law enforcement instructions, remain calm and officers may point guns at you, treat you firmly and question you

Bomb Threats

No matter how ridiculous or implausible the threat may seem during that phone call, all such communications are a crime and should be reported to the police on their emergency number. The vast majority of cases are a hoax and the intent is to cause disruption, fear and/or inconvenience. Any member of staff not just the security department with a direct telephone line, mobile phone or computer could conceivably receive a bomb threat. If you as an operative receive a telephone threat you should:

- ☞ Listen carefully and have immediate access to a pre-written checklist (the best templates are on government websites) on key information that should be recorded

- ☞ Keep the caller talking and alert a colleague to dial the emergency number. If the threat is received via text message do not reply to, forward or delete the message. Note the number of the sender and follow law enforcement advice

- ☞ Know who to contact in your organisation upon receipt of the threat, e.g., building security/senior manager. They will need to assess the threat

Initial assessment of any bomb threat by security management includes:

- ☞ Is the treat part of a series

- ☞ Is there a reason to believe the caller's threat

- ☞ Is the location of the device given precise enough

☞ Could external evacuation move people closer to danger

☞ Is a suspicious device actually visible

Evacuation and Invacuation

Responsibility for the initial decision making remains with the management of the location being threatened. However, the initial call of the type of situation you actually have prompting that, remains with the operative on scene. There should not be a delay in the decision making process whilst waiting for the arrival of police. Police will assess the credibility of the threat at the earliest opportunity they can. All bomb threats reported the police, the police will then want their advice followed accordingly. It is essential that an appropriate plan exists and they should be event and location specific the options are:

Evacuation

☞ Allocate operatives and other specified employees, familiar with evacuation points and assembly (rendezvous) points

☞ At least two assembly points should be identified in opposing directions, and at least 500 metres from the suspicious item, incident or location

☞ Where possible the assembly point should not be a car park

☞ Police will then establish cordons depending upon the size of an identified suspect item

Invacuation (internal or inwards evacuation)

☞ There are occasions when it is safer to remain inside with internal protected spaces when it is known that a bomb is not within or immediately adjacent to your building

☞ If the suspect item is outside your venue people may be exposed to greater danger if the evacuation route inadvertently takes them past the item

☞ When there is a decision made to neither evacuate or invacuate inform staff to search their own immediate vicinities to make sure everything is in order. The best employees to search an area are those that work in that space on a daily basis.

Essentials

➤ **For a standard building evacuation – please leave the facility immediately sir/madam**

➤ **Delivered mail items may be explosive, incendiary, contain sharps, blades or chemical, biological, or radiological material**

➤ **If you think you have something that requires full-scale attendance of police, fire and medical personnel you have a major incident. So always remember METHANE**

➤ **For suspicious items remember the 5W's and the 3C's and for the Stay Safe remember the Run – Hide – Tell**

- As the call taker for a bomb threat always have a pre-written checklist for questions and answers easily accessible in your control room

- There are occasions when it is safer to remain inside your building with internal protected spaces when it is known that a bomb is not within or immediately adjacent to your building

CHAPTER 13

Terrorism and Counter terrorism

This section will give you additional knowledge on the main aspects of terrorism and counterterrorism but also information imbedded into the background of for example, why people turn to terrorism why they still favour just the gun and the bomb and why counterterrorism intelligence is more than just stopping a bomb exploding. This will help put terrorism as we see it today into the context of things we do not always think or talk about. I have simplified these aspects to give you a more rounded view of the subject matter.

Terrorism

There is no universal agreement on the definition of terrorism. Various legal systems and government agencies use different definitions. Moreover, governments have been reluctant to formulate a legally binding and agreed upon definition. It has been argued that this is for three main reasons. Its meaning has historically changed over time, academics cannot agree on it and terrorism is not entirely dissimilar from other forms of irregular violence. The word terrorism originated during the French revolution and was seen as a way of helping to bring the ruling classes to account and achieving greater democracy.

Terrorism seems to be used interchangeably with terms such as guerrilla warfare and insurgency. Guerrillas, insurgents and terrorists all employ the same tactics and use many of the same type of weapons. They rely on for example shooting, bombing, kidnappings and hostage situations. You can view it as an escalatory chain with terrorist cells at the bottom. Then guerrillas controlling territory, with some control over part(s) of a population. With insurgents being the most powerful because over time as their support builds, they have the ability to mobilize tens of thousands of people behind them.

Obviously not all terrorist cells evolve into guerrillas or insurgents and this can be due to many factions within a growing terrorist cell who do not agree on the direction of their cause. I will leave it to your further reading to see who the current designated terrorist organisations are. But when researching further on this subject always remember the term that 'one person's terrorist can be another person's freedom fighter.'

Despite the difficulty with definition ten core elements remain and are constant over time that can assist us to achieve a formula for terrorist behaviour:

- ☞ Involves violence or the threat of violence

- ☞ It is political in nature with a political motive

- ☞ The message type they communicate and the audience they are trying to reach

☞ Terrorist activity in the main is planned, premeditated and purposeful

☞ Part of some identifiable chain of command

☞ Wear no military uniform in the real sense

☞ Do not differentiate between their combatants and non-combatants

☞ Generally refers to non-governmental forms of violence

☞ It can occur anywhere, government borders are not respected

☞ Conducted by individuals who then identify to a political ideology or actual organisation

An important starting point for the operative is the legal definition from your own country. In the United Kingdom, the Terrorism Act 2000 defines terrorism as the use or threat of action where:

(The action needs to fall within subsection 2)

☞ The use or threat is designed to influence the government or to intimidate the public or a section of the public and the use or threat is made for the purpose of advancing a political, religious, or ideological cause.

☞ The action will fall within that subsection 2 if it:

☞ Involves serious violence against a person

☞ Involves serious damage to property

☞ Endangers a person's life, other than that of the person committing the action

☞ Creates a serious risk to the health or safety of the public or a section of the public

☞ Is designed seriously to interfere with or seriously to disrupt an electronic system

The Terrorist

As we have seen terrorists, can come from every walk of life. From marginalized people working in menial jobs to people who have long criminal records or juvenile delinquency to people with very solid middle and even upper-class backgrounds with university educations. These people also come from a variety of racial backgrounds. Individuals who once had a passion for other completely non-religious material interests are suddenly transformed into the religiously devout with committed and determined terrorist aspirations. In looking at the terrorist we must disregard this diversity of background as they are all at some point in their lives dissatisfied with life, in whatever aspect. From this psychologists have developed what they call a Terrorist (six) Staircase Metaphor:

☞ People on the ground floor are trying to make improvements in their life. Individuals become dissatisfied with their lives for different reasons and some of those people then move up to the first floor of the staircase

☞ The theme here is social mobility with individuals trying to make progress in all aspects of their life. Some of these individuals however become very frustrated because they cannot find any routes to making progress because they find their paths blocked for various social and political reasons

☞ Next comes the displacement of aggression. That is to say their view on who is ultimately responsible or to blame, for where they are now in their lives. This is closely linked to what happens next

☞ A disengagement from morality of the majority now takes place. The kind of morality that says killing is wrong and terrorism is wrong. They gradually become engaged with a morality that says under some conditions at least, terrorism is now justified

☞ The process then shifts to categorical thinking. The 'us versus them' mindset. The 'we are right, they are wrong' thinking that allows their enemy to be labelled as non-human, sinful and as anything that justifies exterminating them

☞ Finally, the act of sidestepping inhibitions. Inhibitory mechanisms are in-built within all humans so therefore find it difficult to kill other humans. This stage involves not only labelling the other as non-human and sinful but now perceiving the other as deserving of being the target of aggression for the greater good and for the survival of their ideology

Strategies and Tactics

Terrorists and their strategy is interesting in that often they are not convergent. Terrorist groups use a mix of strategies that at a tactical level are surprisingly more often divorced from strategic success. So for example, a terrorist group undertakes an operation that tries to free hostages and it fails. However, the media attention it attracts and the government response it forces could end up being a strategic success for the terrorist group. The main terrorist strategies:

☞ Attrition - a constant stream of attacks often low level which inflict casualties, destroy property and slowly wear down the other side

☞ Building an insurgency – by gaining the trust of local populations and discrediting their government

☞ Propaganda of the deed - the use of dramatic high profile violence to inspire the population to rise up by dispelling fear of the government, media coverage is key

☞ Spoiling – applies for example, when there is a potential peace negotiation

☞ Lone Wolves - individual terrorists or very small groups acting on their own but inspired by a larger ideology commit violence

From a tactical operation perspective you could argue that despite technological weaponry advances, historically the terrorist still functions in a vacuum. This is important to know as a security operative because of our front-line remit. For well over a century terrorists have continued to rely on the same two basic weapon systems - the gun and the bomb and more recently the moving vehicle on pedestrian walkways. Terrorists generally are not tactically innovative; they rarely deviate from the familiar. From the terrorist point of view the more sophisticated the weapon the more complicated the operation thus the more likely its failure. Terrorists have tended at least historically, to shun weapons or tactics whose success cannot be guaranteed. This tells us something very important about the terrorist mentality that the key characteristic for terrorists is the organisational imperative to succeed.

The reason why is obvious, if the terrorists cannot succeed in an attack, if their weapon(s) or tactics fail they are not going to terrorize anyone. However, they do not have to be terribly sophisticated only clever enough to still access their desired targets. Terrorists continue to rely on what they know will work what they are familiar with and what technologies they have already mastered. Recognising they may not get a second chance to achieve their aims they will typically plan carefully. Generally, the more sophisticated the attack the more complex the attack planning and consequently the greater the information requirement and reconnaissance need but again, surprisingly,

> *Those who conduct reconnaissance generally do not conduct the attack*

The information gathered is typically used by hostiles to assess the state of security and likelihood of detection, to assess vulnerabilities in security and to assess likelihood of success. Understanding hostile reconnaissance in the attack planning process gives security managers a crucial opportunity to disrupt by creating a perception of certain failure by terrorists to attack your facility with success, because of the anti-reconnaissance security activity. This can be achieved because in the process of conducting hostile reconnaissance the terrorists are making themselves vulnerable to detection, which they dislike.

Protective security strategies can therefore be focussed by proactively using the first three parts of the 4D's:

1. Deny – the terrorist the opportunity to gather information

2. Detect – them when they are conducting their reconnaissance

3. Deter – them by promoting failure through messaging and physical demonstration of an effective security presence. This approach will play on the key terrorist concerns of failure and detection

Counter terrorist Intelligence

Preventing a terrorist attack is one of the purposes of counter terrorist intelligence and it has been accomplished in the past on a number of occasions, although it is one of the toughest things that an intelligence service has to try to do. But it is not actually the only purpose. Most counter terrorism intelligence actually gets into many other things:

☞ Strategic intelligence warnings – what are the terrorists plans in terms of entire countries, cities or particular targets such as embassies or military installations

☞ Specific individuals/terrorist cells - collecting information on names, telephone numbers, travel of individuals, their contacts, their movements and importantly their financing

☞ Assisting diplomats – what a cell is doing in a foreign country and information they can provide to their foreign counterparts in an effort to get the cooperation

☞ Human intelligence - a human agent inserted into a terrorist organisation via clandestine methods and handled by the security services

☞ Signal intelligence - the interception of electronic communications of any sort outside of normal information collection as above

☞ Military action – intelligence providing actual target information for example drone strikes

☞ Analysis and grading of information – sound familiar? Particularly difficult in counter terrorism as they seek to join the dots

☞ Foreign allies - often at the front line of following and monitoring local terrorist individuals, cells and groups. They will have collected a lot of information and have valuable locally based human intelligence as above

In relation to intelligence and security management using it practically, the threat levels used in the UK are particularly helpful in preparing your organisation for national threats and the standby status of your crisis/business continuity plan. Terrorism threat levels are designed to give a broad indication of the likelihood of a terrorist attack. They are based on the assessment of a range of factors:

☞ Current intelligence

☞ Recent events

☞ What is known about terrorist intentions and capabilities

☞ There are five threat levels:

☞ Critical – an attack is expected imminently

☞ Severe – an attack is highly likely

☞ Substantial – an attack is a strong possibility

☞ Moderate – an attack is possible but not likely

☞ Low – an attack is unlikely

However, the assessment is generic and does not identify any particular public or business sector or details of location or time. The Government Response Levels (GRL) provides a general indication of the protective security measures that should be applied at any time. They are informed by the threat level but also consider specific assessments of risk and vulnerability. There are three levels of response - exceptional, heightened, and normal. Response levels equate to threat levels and tend to relate to sites, whereas threat levels usually just relate to broad areas of activity. There are a variety of site specific security measures that can be applied within each response level. Response levels should remain confidential within any overall security plan. The following are threat levels and security response levels combined and so important to know for your organisation:

- ☞ Critical (imminent) = exceptional maximum protective security measures to meet specific threats and to minimise vulnerability and risk

- ☞ Severe (high) = heightened additional but sustainable severe/substantial protective security measures reflecting the broad nature of the threat combined with specific business and geographical vulnerabilities and judgements on acceptable risk to your organisation

- ☞ Substantial (strong) = as above

- ☞ Moderate (possible) = normal routine protective security. Low and moderate measures appropriate to the business concerned

- ☞ Low (unlikely) = no response level required

Essentials

- There is no universally agreed definition of terrorism due to changes in activity over time, academics unable to agree and because it is not dissimilar to other random acts of violence

- There are ten core elements that remain present that help provide the best formula to define terrorism

- When we are looking at the terrorists, we must dismiss the diversity of their backgrounds and can apply the Terrorist (6) Staircase Metaphor

- Terrorism and strategy is often not convergent and for them tactically the more sophisticated the weapon the more complicated the operation thus the more likely its failure

- Terrorists who conduct the reconnaissance do not generally conduct the attack

- Counter terrorist intelligence generally has eight main tools available with the key ones being human and signal

- The five threat levels are critical, severe, substantial, moderate, and low

- Our threat level aligned security responses will be exceptional, heightened, and normal

CHAPTER 14

Be the 20 in the 80/20

The Best

In this final section I want to introduce you to another favourite concept of mine written and devised by Richard Koch in his books the 80/20 Principle and Living the 80/20 Way. This final section is about you and how you conduct yourself daily to maximise your success generally and as a security operative. The idea of his books is for people to create more doing less and to effectively focus on your best 20 percent.

Koch's premise is that 80 percent of results come from only 20 percent of our efforts. Or put another way 80 percent of what we want, what is important, only actually comes from 20 percent of what we do. Koch states, for example, that 20 percent of retail staff make 80 percent of sales. 20 percent of media stars have more than 80 percent of the coverage and 20 percent of scientists have more than 80 percent of the breakthroughs etc. etc. Thus, only a very few things we do really matter. I will leave these points here and recommend you read it yourself and now tell you why it is a brilliant philosophy that the security operative working shifts should embrace.

For you in your work as a security operative (or other occupation) your personal circumstances are always different from everybody else, even though the work we do and the processes daily are the same and very methodical. But what we can all do to enhance our standard of security work is to also try and simplify our lives. By that I mean the essence of this book is about basics so the less we concentrate on numerous outside activities and minimise them, the more we can undertake our security work to a higher level. Now that is not to say let your life revolve around security work. But as we spend 50 percent of our lives at work - and there is no way around that - just consider simplifying other areas of your life. As Koch suggests, put work on one side of the paper and your personal life on the other and see if you can thin down your activities so you conduct your life in a way that you can achieve maximum results.

However you do it, just remember to undertake your work as a security operative in a manner that you are the best that you can be. For example, look at people that are the best in their chosen field of expertise. I say expertise because remember if you have many years of experience at your facility and/or other academic knowledge relating to security you are indeed an expert in your field. Simply because you have knowledge of your facility that many others do not. When I say be the best you can be, look at other people. People like Warren Buffet the investor, Gordon Ramsey in cooking and broadcasting, Jodie Foster in filmmaking and directing, Tom Brady the Quarterback, Simone Biles the gymnast or Ronaldo the soccer player. Just look at individuals in their field that are always operating at a higher level and make sure that you are being the best you possibly can be, so always try and be the 20 in the 80/20.

The Basics

In your work as security operative use the BASICS concept:

- ☞ Brevity – use concise words and explanations

- ☞ Application – of knowledge to your work, learning, (and life)

- ☞ Summarize – the main points in discussion

- ☞ Integrate – knowledge with your daily practices

- ☞ Competent – in your own ability and knowledge

- ☞ Surpass – be greater than your peers in your work

- ☞ Here are two quotes to remember when things look like they are getting complicated in the security world:

- ☞ 'Simplicity is the ultimate sophistication.' - Leonardo da Vinci

- ☞ 'I believe most things can be said in a few lines.' - Enzo Ferrari (F1Racing)

Here is a list you should remember to help keep you on track with your personal life and as a professional security operative:

☞ Make your bed – the first task of the day leads to another and another...

☞ Have a Blueprint – of where you want to go in any area

☞ Define success for yourself

☞ Do not leave crumbs – if you do bad things, they will catch up with you

☞ Respect everyone

☞ Life is not fair, move on

☞ Do not be afraid to fail

☞ Take risks

☞ Lift up the downtrodden

☞ Never, ever ring the bell – give up

The Asset

Make no mistake as a security operative sleep can be your prime number one personal asset, or it can assist in your downfall. As someone who spent the best part of twenty years working a twenty-four hour shift pattern of early, late and night shifts, before you think about your diet or your exercise regime or any other form of relaxation, if this is not your priority everything else will be a completely false economy. Sleep expert Matthew Walker has come up with some scientifically based reasons why sleep is so important and for the likes of shift workers this is factual gold dust.

Walker states that sleep is mother nature's best effort yet at immortality and twenty five to thirty years is the cumulative time that most humans will spend sleeping during their lifetimes. So, let's start out with some interesting facts about how people sleep and blow away a few myths at the same time, first the bad:

- ☞ Those that tell you they can get by on five hours sleep every night – they are one in four million

- ☞ After nineteen hours without sleep your cognitive impairment is equal to being legally drunk

- ☞ Humans are the only mammals that willingly delay going to sleep

- ☞ Six hundred extra calories consumed by under slept participants in a study, sounds familiar to me in the police and security world

- ☞ Two hundred percent increase in the likelihood of heart attack or stroke in the over 45's sleeping fewer than six hours

- ☞ 1.2 million is an estimated number of annual car accidents caused by sleepiness in the US

Now the good:

- ☞ You need between seven and a half and nine hours sleep per night, non-negotiable. Only you will know where you need to be in between that timescale

☞ Find a sleep routine, go to bed at the same time including days off because your body clock is a crucial player in your sleep pattern

☞ Eat and drink light and cut out cardio activity in the hours preceding sleep time

☞ Cut out caffeine and nicotine way before bedtime

☞ Check your device at the bedroom door no blue light, it blocks brain sleep chemicals

☞ Leave yourself to slowly unwind before bedtime

Methods and Sources

This book has been put together for the most part, using my skills and experience obtained during my police and current security career, by practical application of experience in uniform policing services as well as the investigation of volume crime and plain clothes operations. Within the security industry, experience from the police environment is extremely useful, however I found it more beneficial and productive not to be blinkered by that police knowledge and experience, to the detriment of what is in reality a whole new world of experience in security as well as new and exciting learning. I have sought in my second career to apply all the best aspects of policing to promote better ways of working by the security operative and in turn to promote a high level of customer satisfaction and increased risk management. I have always sought to simplify the subject matter but provide scope for further reading using similar sources to those listed.

There are a number of sources used in this book, primarily the UK government department website the Centre for the Protection of National Infrastructure (CPNI.) This is an extremely valuable resource for the UK security operative that covers a multitude of security aspects. Please reference similar resources for wherever you are in the world. In the sections one to seven sources include CPNI, the International Organisation for Standardisation (ISO), the British Security Industry Association (BSIA), the Information Commissioners Office

(ICO), the Institute of Lighting Professionals, Tim Crowe for CPTED theory, Nassim Nicholas Taleb, UK government legislation and handbooks from the UK Security Industry Authority (SIA.) Sections eight to fifteen include CPNI, BBC News, the World Health Organisation (WHO), Jonathan Bernstein, Gavin Robertson and Andy Cook, Bruce Hoffman, Daniel Byman, Fathali Moghaddam and Paul Pillar. The concluding section used the sources of Richard Koch and Matthew Walker, the sleep scientist.